Oxford Reading Tree

Roder

Teacher's Handbook

STAGES 1–9

Compiled by
Catherine Baker and Thelma Page

OXFORD
UNIVERSITY PRESS

OXFORD
UNIVERSITY PRESS

is a department of the University of Oxford.
It furthers the University's objective of excellence in research, scholarship, and education by publishing worldwide in

Oxford New York
Auckland Cape Town Dar es Salaam Hong Kong Karachi
Kuala Lumpur Madrid Melbourne Mexico City Nairobi
New Delhi Shanghai Taipei Toronto

With offices in

Argentina Austria Brazil Chile Czech Republic France Greece
Guatemala Hungary Italy Japan Poland Portugal Singapore
South Korea Switzerland Thailand Turkey Ukraine Vietnam

First published 2008

Written by Catherine Baker and Thelma Page
based on the original characters created by Roderick Hunt and Alex Brychta

British Library Cataloguing in Publication Data

Data available

ISBN: 978-0-19-846706-9

10 9 8 7 6 5 4 3 2 1

Cover illustration by Alex Brychta

Inside illustrations by Alex Brychta

Page make-up by Q2A Media

Printed in the UK by Ashford Colour Press

Paper used in the production of this book is a natural, recyclable product made from wood grown in sustainable forests. The manufacturing process conforms to the environmental regulations of the country of origin.

Contents

Welcome to Oxford Reading Tree!

Introducing the family

We are the Robinson family:

Dad

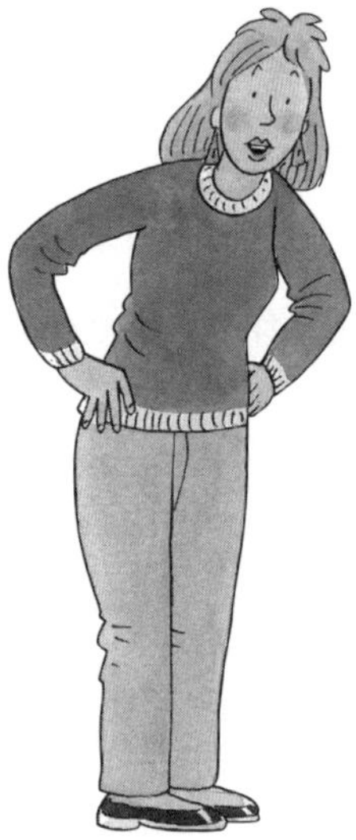

Mum

Chip

Biff

Kipper

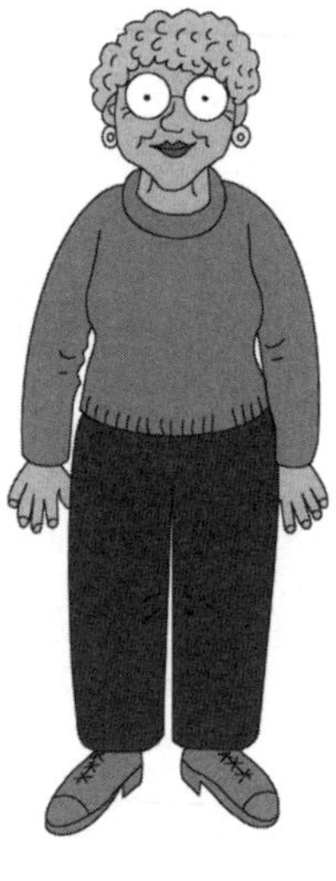

Gran

Floppy

We are best friends of the Robinson children:

Wilf and Wilma

Nadim

Anneena

Dad likes playing with the children, so I do lots of the jobs around the house.
Mum can't wait to fix things, and she is better at it than me. So all the tools in the house belong to Mum.
Biff and I are twins. Biff is great fun but don't give Biff anything to hold, she might drop it.
Chip is a great brother most of the time. He is very careful, so if you want something drawn or painted, ask Chip to do it.
I love spending time with the children. I don't think Mum and Dad completely trust me not to get into trouble though.
They say I am mischievous, whatever that means. Gran is my favourite visitor. We always have fun with Gran.
My job is to look after the family. Sometimes they are not very clever. I see things happening long before they do.

The author is Roderick Hunt

When his own sons were young, Rod found it hard to interest them in reading. He sympathised because nothing interesting ever happened in the books they brought home. Rod has remedied this situation in a remarkable way by writing stories where something interesting, funny and believable happens in every one, however short the story. Motivating children to read is not a problem with Oxford Reading Tree.

Children learn to read through stories. At the early stages all the stories are based on everyday experiences. A sense of involvement with the story and the characters stimulates children to talk with confidence. The words on the page match their language; reading makes sense from the very first book. The stories provide a context in which children are ready to learn basic reading skills: how letters, words and sentences combine to create meaning.

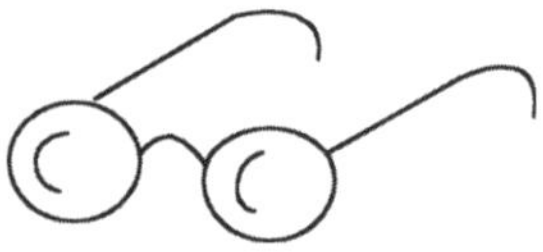

The illustrator is Alex Brychta

Alex has developed the style of illustration that has become the trademark of Oxford Reading Tree. There is always more detail than strictly necessary in every picture. Observant children soon notice that a dog is often somewhere in the landscape and that most stories have a pair of spectacles seemingly abandoned in odd locations. Alex tells children a story that explains both these additions:

I often go to a park where there is a notice saying 'Dogs must be kept on the lead'. I nearly always meet a dog off the lead, so clearly the dog is too short-sighted to read the notice. So I buy old pairs of spectacles from junk shops and when I meet a dog in the park I put a pair of spectacles on him. Of course, he shakes his head and they drop off sooner or later, so that is why there are pairs of spectacles in odd places in my pictures.

How Rod and Alex work together

Rod begins a new story by sitting in a comfortable chair and staring at the ceiling. Visualising the whole story from beginning to end is essential before he begins to write. The visualisation process might take days, but after that the writing is easy. After the text has been edited and trialled in schools, Rod talks through the story with Alex. He explains exactly what is happening on each page. Sometimes Alex will say, 'But I see it like this...' and draw a different perspective. At this stage much of the humour, and running jokes (the nosy neighbour, the cross short-sighted gentleman) are included. And so another story takes shape.

You can meet Roderick Hunt and Alex Brychta on the video clips on the Oxford Reading Tree *MagicPage CD-ROMs*.

What is special about Oxford Reading Tree?

Captivating both children and adults

All the stories are fun to read, often having a surprise ending. The illustrations add humorous and interesting details. Observant children will find lots of visual jokes and details to delight them. (Adults will notice even more!)

Reflecting children's everyday lives in the twenty-first century

Oxford Reading Tree engages children's attention at every stage because the things that happen to Biff, Chip and Kipper are happening to them: the first day at school; the first loose tooth; quarrelling with your sister; getting told off for messing up new shoes.

Inspiring imagination

The magic key stories from Stage 5 onwards open up all kinds of possibilities through magic adventures. There is just enough danger to make it exciting, with the assurance that the key will glow and all will be well.

Fit for a modern curriculum

With its wide range of resources, Oxford Reading Tree helps you deliver the most up to date curriculum, easily. It is ideal for developing skills in speaking and listening, word recognition and phonics, and language comprehension.

A clearly structured progression

Oxford Reading Tree stages gradually progress from the wordless stories about Biff, Chip and Kipper at Stage 1 and the *Big Talkabout Cards,* to Stage 9 with a gradual increase in the amount of text, number of pages, and complexity of sentences and plot. This progression is mirrored in the phonics teaching programme, *Songbirds*, the non-fiction *Fireflies*, the variety fiction strand *Snapdragons* and the poetry strand *Glow-worms*.

New stories keep it fresh

New stories are being added all the time to enrich each stage and provide plenty of practice. New materials are always trialled extensively in schools to ensure that they meet the needs of the children and the teachers in the classrooms of today. Teachers' comments are always taken into account when developing stories and materials.

Encouraging children to talk

Oxford Reading Tree is based on talk. Extended stories in the early stages encourage children to contribute as the story is told or read. The situations and adventures encourage children to talk about their own ideas and memories. Speaking and listening opportunities arise naturally from each story. Children are involved and motivated, keen to contribute.

Extensive support materials

There is an extensive range of materials to support:

- lesson planning (*Teaching Notes*, *Guided Reading Cards*)
- independent and group activities (*Games*, *Story CDs*, *Playscripts,* photocopy materials such as *Group Activity Sheets* and *Comprehension*)
- home liaison (notes inside book covers).

The characters do not become dated

The children's names, Biff, Chip and Kipper, do not link them to a decade or a particular fashion. The names Biff, Chip and Kipper derive from Kipper's early attempts to say names when he was learning to talk. Biff is really Beth, Chip is really David and Kipper is really Christopher, but these real names are not used in any of the stories.

Some fascinating facts about Oxford Reading Tree

- Rod and Alex have written 306 books so far about the adventures of Biff, Chip and Kipper, and the number continues to rise.
- Alex often uses people he knows as models for characters. In *Roman Adventure* (Stage 7) Rod appears as Caesar, while Alex is the chariot driver, Mark.
- Alex is not keen on drawing horses, so in *Rotten Apples* (Stage 7), Harry Smith's horse is nearly always entering or leaving the scene, keeping illustrations of the entire animal to a minimum.
- Rod's son also likes to write stories. David Hunt has written several books including *The Big Breakfast* (Stage 7) and *Olympic Adventure* (Stage 6).
- Oxford Reading Tree's appeal is so wide that it has been translated into many languages, including Spanish and Korean! It is available in 133 countries and has even been translated into Braille.
- Gran is often in more trouble than the children. She deflates a bouncy castle in *Castle Adventure* (Stage 5), breaks a window in *A Day in London* and later in the story has to leave the waxworks exhibition in disgrace.
- Jokes that parents notice and enjoy more than children include: the barbecue that refuses to light in *The Barbecue* (Stage 3) and the inept but willing babysitter in *The Babysitter*.
- There are often jokes in posters and trade names, for instance paint comes from 'Tatibah' (*Come In!* Stage 4) and the children go to 'Ortree Primary school' (*Green Island*, Stage 9).
- Alex's son, Dylan, drew the artwork for *Kipper's Diary* (Stage 1+) when he was just 6 years old!
- Oxford Reading Tree is over 22 years old. First published in 1985, it has continued to respond to teacher's needs and is still as popular as ever!

How Oxford Reading Tree works for you

Oxford Reading Tree and the simple view of reading

Following the renewal of the Primary National Strategy *Literacy Framework* in 2006, a new simple view of reading has been introduced, with an emphasis on two core areas for developing children's literacy skills: **word recognition** (phonics and high frequency words) and **language comprehension**. The renewed *Literacy Framework* also gives a higher profile to speaking and listening skills, and reinforces the importance of embedding reading within a broad and rich curriculum.

All of these changes fit perfectly with the Oxford Reading Tree philosophy, and now more than ever, Oxford Reading Tree can help you deliver all the requirements of the literacy curriculum.

Word recognition

Phonics

The simple view of reading recommends systematic phonics teaching, enhanced by a wide variety of good quality readers, from the earliest stages of reading.

- Oxford Reading Tree *Songbirds* is a complete synthetic phonics programme which meets all the required criteria for high-quality phonics teaching. The fun and fully decodable stories are levelled to Oxford Reading Tree stages, and the *eSongbirds* interactive whiteboard software enables you to teach the whole class using a multi-sensory approach.
- *Floppy's Phonics* is a new series of real Biff, Chip and Kipper stories that are fully decodable for focused phonics practice.
- The Biff, Chip and Kipper stories also offer many additional opportunities to reinforce children's phonic skills and knowledge.

High frequency words

- All Oxford Reading Tree stories are written using a mix of high frequency decodable and tricky words, so children get plenty of practice with recognising high frequency words that do not necessarily conform to phonic rules.
- Resources such as the *Context Cards* help you give children practice recognising high frequency words both in and out of context.

Case study

Jane Langrell, Literacy Co-ordinator at Canning Street Primary School, Newcastle, says:

"As teachers we feel confident that if children work through the early stages systematically, they will get to know a wide range of 'tricky' words as well as learning how to read decodable words."

Language comprehension

Within the simple view of reading, language comprehension is of equal importance to word recognition.

- Oxford Reading Tree *MagicPage* allows you to teach children how to read. It offers comprehension alongside phonics and speaking and listening in the context of your favourite Biff, Chip and Kipper stories on the interactive whiteboard. It is the perfect tool for putting Oxford Reading Tree into the heart of your classroom.
- The Biff, Chip and Kipper books offer even the youngest readers a real experience of multilayered stories, well-developed characters and rewarding plots which will keep them hooked. As children enjoy the stories they are actively predicting, visualising and engaging with the stories.
- *Snapdragons* are picture books written by many leading children's authors. The variety of fiction allows children to practise comprehension skills while reading a range of different types of fiction.
- *Fireflies* are exciting non-fiction books in a range of text types and topics to engage and extend children's reading skills.
- A range of teaching support materials such as *Teaching Notes*, *Comprehension Photocopy Masters*, *Group Activity Sheets*, *Workbooks* and *Games* related to the stories will also help you enhance children's comprehension skills.

Speaking and listening

The renewed *Literacy Framework* acknowledges the central role played by speaking and listening in developing literacy skills.

- Oxford Reading Tree *MagicPage CD-ROM* software for your interactive whiteboard helps bring the Biff, Chip and Kipper books alive, providing wonderful stimulus material such as images, film clips and audio, to get children talking and listening purposefully.
- The *Big Talkabout Cards* and *Big Books* are ideal to encourage class discussions about the characters and to help children develop skills of prediction, visualisation and empathy.
- The Biff, Chip and Kipper stories have always offered a wonderful range of multi-layered storylines, and the funny illustrations encourage children to talk about and explore the stories together. Speaking and listening activities form an integral part of the *Teaching Notes* for each story.

Writing

Oxford Reading Tree provides a motivating and familiar context for developing children's early writing skills.

- The Biff, Chip and Kipper stories provide a familiar context within which children will love writing their own stories about the characters.
- There are writing activities suggested in the *Teaching Notes* that accompany each of the stories.
- Oxford Reading Tree *MagicPage* offers great stimulus materials for shared writing, including the capacity to write your own class version of each featured story, and plenty of follow-up ideas for individual and group writing, as well as accompanying practice books.

- *Routes to Writing* is a dedicated writing programme for Key Stage 1 which has been specially developed to sit alongside Oxford Reading Tree, with books levelled to the Oxford Reading Tree stages that offer models of writing at children's own reading age.

Case study

Rachel Crouch, Headteacher at St Nicholas' Primary School, Oxford, says:

"At the Foundation Stage we especially enjoy the wordless stories, where children create and stick their own sentences to the pages, to make their own story. This gives a great sense of ownership."

Meeting the needs of all your children

Oxford Reading Tree contains a wide variety of resources that will help you support your less able readers, and extend the skills of the more able. The structure and breadth of the programme ensure that there is a choice of appropriate books to engage children at every stage of their reading development. There are detailed lists of resources within the 'Stage by stage planning charts' section in this *Teacher's Handbook* (pages 41 to 86). They suggest resources for children needing more pracice and resources for further reading. The following resources will also be helpful:

- *Patterned Stories* and *First Sentences* (Stages 1+ and 2) provide practise of high frequency vocabulary.
- *Floppy's Phonics* (Stage 1+ to Stage 6) provide focused phonics practice.
- *Sparrows* (Stages 3 and 4) extend the range of characters and settings children meet – helpful for children who need more breadth of reading experience but are not quite ready to move up to the higher stages.
- *Robins* provide 18 extension stories for more able infant readers, and they are book banded at levels Turquoise to White.
- *Jackdaws* anthologies provide 24 extension readers for your most able readers and include fiction and non-fiction. They are book banded.
- Oxford Reading Tree *All Stars* provide 36 quality chapter books to appeal to your most able infant readers, at Year 1 and Year 2.

A rich and broad curriculum

With Oxford Reading Tree at the heart of your classroom you can be sure of offering children breadth and richness as part of their reading experience.

- Oxford Reading Tree *MagicPage CD-ROMs* include fascinating links to the wider world beyond the story, including cross-curricular videos.
- *Snapdragons* and *Fireflies* help to ensure that children encounter a very wide range of different types of fiction and non-fiction.
- You can use the very best of trade children's fiction and non-fiction alongside your Oxford Reading Tree books so that children develop an appetite for a wide range of reading.

Assessment for Learning and personalisation

Assessment for Learning, or AfL, is a way of involving children in the whole cycle of teaching and learning through:

- activating prior knowledge
- sharing and making their own learning intentions
- understanding where they are on the way to reaching the learning intention
- having a clear set of success criteria so that they know what the outcome of their learning should look like
- identifying what they need to learn and do next.

AfL is a central part of the Oxford Reading Tree philosophy. The guidance for this and for involving your children in their learning are:

- Assessment focuses and Primary National Strategy objectives for every book (listed in the *Teaching Notes* booklets accompanying each pack).

Objective Read some high frequency words (5.9).

On page 4, ask children to find 'his'. How did they know which word it was? Talk about the strategy used. If necessary, model segmenting into phonemes ('h–i–s') and match each phoneme with the letters on the page.

Assessment *(R, AF1)* Can children find the word 'his' in a collection of flashcards, or among other words written on the board?

- Self-assessment features for children to use on the *Comprehension Photocopy Masters*.

How did I do? 

- Integrated AfL features accompanying every story activity in Oxford Reading Tree *MagicPage*.

Assessment for Learning

Learning Intention: *We are learning to spell simple words.*

Suggested Success Criteria:

- I can sound out letters in words in order.
- I can match sounds to letter shapes.
- I can blend letters together to make words.

Talk Partner: *Can you find the pictures of the words we have been looking at in the story?*

- The *I Can* books in Oxford Reading Tree *MagicPage* provide a personal record book for every child, giving a really engaging opportunity for children to be fully involved in their own learning.

Oxford Reading Tree overview chart

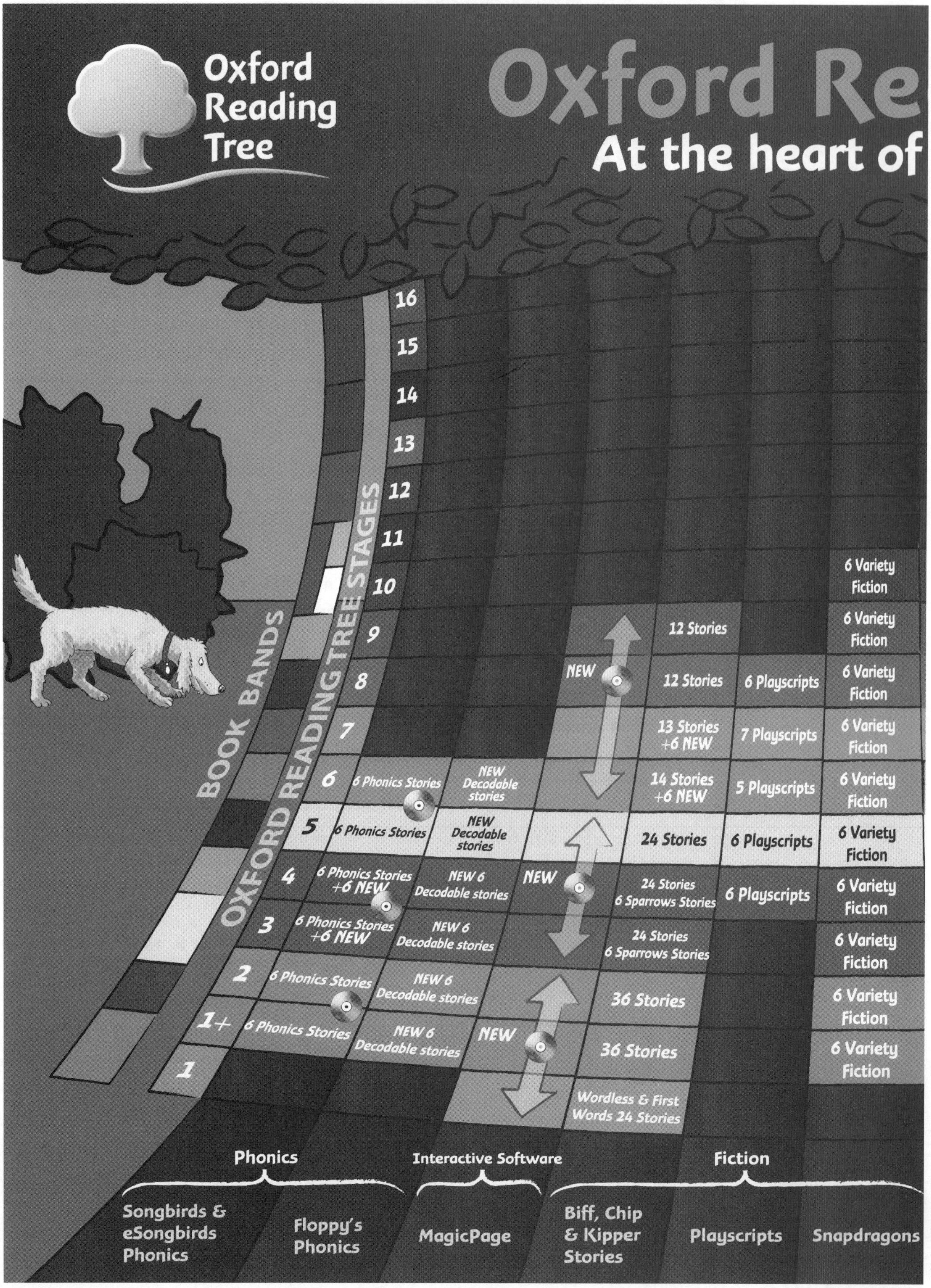

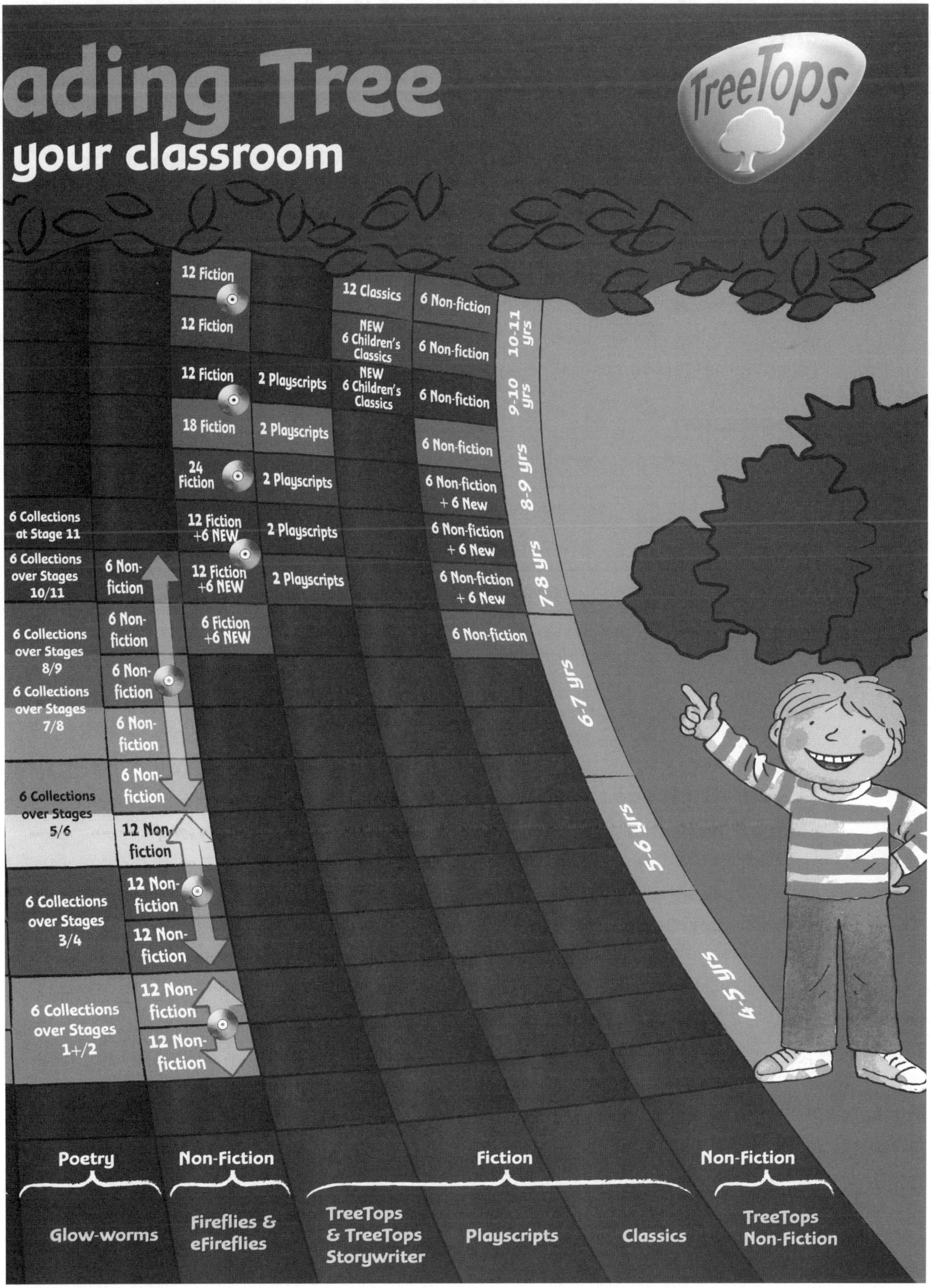
ading Tree
your classroom
TreeTops
12 Fiction
12 Fiction
12 Fiction
18 Fiction
24 Fiction
12 Fiction +6 NEW
12 Fiction +6 NEW
6 Fiction +6 NEW
2 Playscripts
2 Playscripts
2 Playscripts
2 Playscripts
2 Playscripts
12 Classics
NEW 6 Children's Classics
NEW 6 Children's Classics
6 Non-fiction
6 Non-fiction
6 Non-fiction
6 Non-fiction
6 Non-fiction + 6 New
6 Non-fiction + 6 New
6 Non-fiction + 6 New
6 Non-fiction
10-11 yrs
9-10 yrs
8-9 yrs
7-8 yrs
6-7 yrs
5-6 yrs
4-5 yrs
6 Collections at Stage 11
6 Collections over Stages 10/11
6 Collections over Stages 8/9
6 Collections over Stages 7/8
6 Collections over Stages 5/6
6 Collections over Stages 3/4
6 Collections over Stages 1+/2
6 Non-fiction
6 Non-fiction
6 Non-fiction
6 Non-fiction
6 Non-fiction
12 Non-fiction
12 Non-fiction
12 Non-fiction
12 Non-fiction
12 Non-fiction
Poetry
Non-Fiction
Fiction
Non-Fiction
Glow-worms
Fireflies & eFireflies
TreeTops & TreeTops Storywriter
Playscripts
Classics
TreeTops Non-Fiction

Teaching reading with Oxford Reading Tree

Matching the recommendations of the simple view of reading

The simple view of reading describes the need for confident and competent word recognition skills alongside the ability to understand any text genre. The recommendation is that phonic work should be time limited, giving children the skills to decode text from an early age. Comprehension, on the other hand, is an ongoing skill, developing constantly throughout life. In choosing Oxford Reading Tree you are providing for both elements.

- *Songbirds* provides systematic support for teaching phonics.
- *Floppy's Phonics* provides fun phonics practice with Biff, Chip and Kipper.
- Oxford Reading Tree *MagicPage* and the core Biff, Chip and Kipper stories provide lots of opportunities for language comprehension.

Together these resources will help you teach every child how to read.

Progression

As a general guide many schools use the stages in the following year groups.

	England/Wales	Northern Ireland	Age
Stages 1, 1+, 2	Year R	Y1/P1	4–5
Stages 3, 4, 5	Year 1	Y2/P2	5–6
Stages 6, 7, 8, 9	Year 2	Y3/P3	6–7

Books across all the genres can be interwoven at each stage. *Songbirds*, *Fireflies*, *Snapdragons* and *Glow-worms* poetry are all matched to the same stages as the core Biff, Chip and Kipper books.

In Year R (Stages 1, 1+ and 2)
Shared reading and writing, speaking and listening

From the first day in the Reception class (P1), the *Big Talkabout Cards* and the *Big Books* provide a format for shared conversation. In describing what they see happening on these large format cards and storybooks, children quickly make links to their own lives, and contribute freely to discussions. They learn to listen to each other, to wait their turn, and to express their own ideas. A rich understanding is supported by the extended versions of the stories at the early stages, and suggested questions about the text elicit responses requiring different levels and types of comprehension.

Using Oxford Reading Tree *MagicPage* with Reception classes enables you to introduce children to shared reading, writing, and speaking and listening activities based on the familiar core characters, Biff, Chip and Kipper. Oxford Reading Tree *MagicPage CD-ROM Stages 1-2* uses well-loved stories from Stages 1, 1+ and 2 as a starting point for speaking and listening, phonics, comprehension and writing activities, as well as cross-curricular videos that link the stories to the wider world.

Word Recognition

Songbirds is a structured phonics teaching programme which introduces all the phonemes in English to children in six progressive stages. You can use the *eSongbirds* interactive whiteboard software and the lively decodable stories to teach and practise phonics at each stage.

Floppy's Phonics sit alongside *Songbirds*. They can be used to support the phonics teaching of *Songbirds* in the familiar context of the well-loved Oxford Reading Tree characters

Both *Songbirds* and *Floppy's Phonics* follow the teaching progression of the National Primary Strategy *Letters and Sounds*. They are both supported by notes for parents on the inside covers of the stories and by free *Teaching Notes* booklets.

Tricky words

Oxford Reading Tree stories are based upon a carefully graded core vocabulary of high frequency words. Reading the stories ensures that the children become thoroughly familiar with the 'tricky words'. There are plenty of support materials, such as *Context Cards, Games* boxes and photocopiable work sheets to encourage practice in an enjoyable and meaningful way.

Language comprehension

The stories at Stages 1 and 2 are mainly about the Robinson family (Biff, Chip, Kipper, Mum, Dad and Gran), with lots of stories centred on Kipper, who at 4–5 years old is just like the children in Year R. Children find it easy to relate to and understand the sequence of events. They will have had similar experiences, so you can encourage them to make inferences and deductions about the story and the characters from the earliest stages.

Activities suggested in the *Teaching Notes* support all aspects of comprehension. For instance comprehension activities based on *New Trainers* (Stage 2) include:

Group or guided reading

Introducing the book

- C *(Questioning)* Read the title and look at the picture. *Who has new trainers?*
- C *(Prediction)* Ask the children to say what might happen to the new shoes.
- C *(Questioning)* Look through the book to see what happened to the new trainers. Ask: *Where did Chip go to play? What happened to the new trainers? Who was cross with Chip? What happened to Dad at the end of the story?*

- C *(Summarising)* Ask children to explain why Dad is cross at the end of the story.

- C *(Clarifying)* Look back through the pages and ask the children if there are any questions they would like to ask any of the characters. Discuss possible answers.

Apart from the *Teaching Notes* there is a range of other materials to support the development of comprehension skills including *Comprehension Photocopy Masters* for group and individual work, and interactive activities in Oxford Reading Tree *MagicPage* and *Oxford Reading Tree Online*.

In Year 1 (Stages 3, 4 and 5)

Broadly, children in Year 1 (P2) will be using Stages 3–5, although of course some will have moved further ahead and others will still be at earlier stages. These divisions are therefore just a guide.

Shared reading and writing, speaking and listening

Just as the children's world begins to expand to include a greater focus on friends, holidays and school, so the stories also have wider horizons. Shared experiences remain central to the stories, continuing the expectation that children will relate to the events and comment on them.

The magic key

Stage 4 extends the stories further as events lead to the discovery of the magic key after a storm. In Stage 5 the key begins to glow, and extraordinary things begin to happen to the children. This magic device introduces an element of fantasy and adventure, and the thought that anything might happen! Stories become more exhilarating and meet children's need for excitement and unexpected situations. This encourages greater speculation and more creative predictions, as well as providing opportunities for children to empathise with the characters.

Just as at Reception, Oxford Reading Tree *MagicPage CD-ROM Stages 3-5* for Year 1 offers opportunities for whole-class shared reading, writing, speaking and listening based on the core Biff, Chip and Kipper stories at Stages 3, 4, and 5.

Word recognition

Songbirds at Stages 3–6, introduce more complex phonic patterns and *Floppy's Phonics* continue to provide revision and further practice. Structured notes on the inside covers of the stories enable children to be supported at home and by helpers in school. *Teaching Notes* on each story give more detailed support.

Tricky words

Highly predictable text in the Biff, Chip and Kipper stories at Stages 3–5 enables children to recognise and practice high frequency words in an enjoyable and meaningful context.

Language comprehension

The structure of the *Teaching Notes* continue to support the different strategies for comprehension: prediction, questioning, summarising, clarifying and imagining. The different aspects of comprehension are also taught through the *Comprehension Photocopy Masters* for these stages.

In Year 2 (Stages 6, 7, 8, and 9)

In general, children in Year 2 (P3) will be reading Stages 6–9, although some may be at earlier stages and others will have moved ahead to enjoy *Robins* Packs 1, 2, and 3, *Jackdaws* Packs 1, 2 and 3, *All Stars* Packs 1 to 3a and *TreeTops* Stages 9–16.

Shared reading and writing, speaking and listening

Just as in Reception and Year 1, the resources for Year 2 allow you to teach shared reading and writing, and speaking and listening in a supportive and familiar context. Oxford Reading Tree *MagicPage Stages 6-9* provides stimulus material for speaking and listening, writing, reading and comprehension activities focused on popular books from Stages 6, 7, 8 and 9.

The magic key

In Stages 6–9 the magic adventures take the children further out into the world, and they begin to explore historical events and meet people from the past and from other cultures. These stories in particular provide many opportunities for links to other subject areas and make it easy for literacy activities to be central to cross-curricular planning. At these stages there are also some adventures focusing on everyday issues that do not involve the magic key, such as *The Motorway* (Stage 7), or *Green Island* (Stage 9).

Word recognition

The books at Stages 6–9 build on skills and vocabulary which children have acquired in the earlier stages, continuing to build up reading stamina and confidence in a gradual step-by-step way. The *Teaching Notes* give guidance on assessing and reinforcing children's word recognition skills, including phonic skills and the ability to decode tricky words that do not completely conform to phonic rules.

Language comprehension

Once again the *Teaching Notes* provide full support for the range of comprehension skills and strategies. The *Comprehension Photocopy Masters* for Stages 6–9 also provide further practice for children as individuals or in groups. In addition, Oxford Reading Tree *MagicPage* includes many activities that will enhance children's comprehension skills.

Features throughout all stages:

Assessment for learning

The *Teaching Notes* for each book support assessment by giving clear assessment statements, usually headed 'Check the children can...'. These are based on the QCA Assessment Focuses for reading and writing.

QCA Assessment Focuses for Reading

Assessment Check that children:

- *(R, AF1)* track text matching letters to sounds
- *(R, AF1)* use phonic knowledge to sound out and blend the phonemes in words, particularly the phonic words (see chart on page 4)
- *(R, AF2)* use their understanding of the story and their own experiences to explain the illustrations and the main events.

QCA Assessment Focuses for Writing

Assessment *(W, AF1)* Did the children attempt to write without help? Did they have ideas for notices they would need?

Oxford Reading Tree *MagicPage* has been created with the Assessment for Learning principles in mind, with learning intentions and success criteria written in child-friendly language to enable children to participate in their learning actively and assess their own progress. Children are encouraged during shared or independent work to respond with thumb signals (thumbs up, down or sideways) to say how well they feel they understand the concepts.

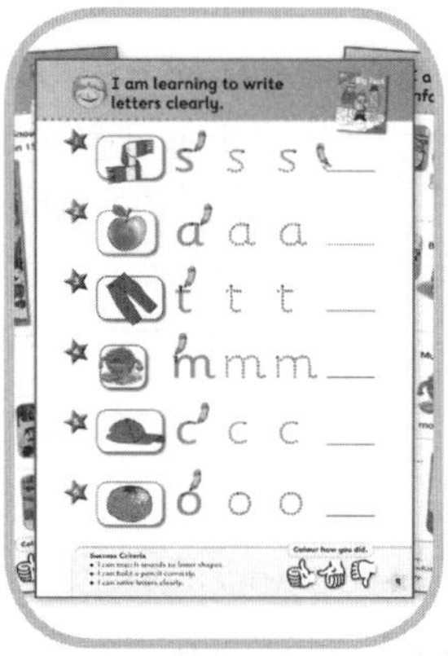

Assessment for Learning

Learning Intention: *We are learning to spell simple words.*

Suggested Success Criteria:

- I can sound out letters in words in order.
- I can match sounds to letter shapes.
- I can blend letters together to make words.

Talk Partner: *Can you find the pictures of the words we have been looking at in the story?*

Extended Learning: In pairs, children can challenge each other to write the CVC words they have just explored.

The checklists of reading skills provided for each stage in this *Teacher's Handbook* are photocopiable lists of the main reading skills children at each stage should be acquiring. You will also find checklists of all the books, at each stage, which are photocopiable pages for keeping dated group or individual records of books read.

Shared reading

Teaching reading with Oxford Reading Tree is a pleasure because the stories are involving and motivating, and children achieve success. The Biff, Chip and Kipper books are particularly motivating because familiarity with the characters is an excellent starting point for a new text, giving children confidence in tackling a new book.

Guided and group reading

Guided reading groups are easy to organise, supported by the stage and book band level information. The fact that there are different genres (e.g. fiction, non-fiction, poetry) at each level also make it easy to ensure that children are supported and are not expected to move up to the next level before they are ready. Leaders of guided reading groups are supported by detailed suggestions in the *Teaching Notes*, supplied free with every pack of six books. These notes reduce the amount of preparation time required of the teacher, and also enable students and other classroom staff to support a group of young readers with confidence.

Independent reading

The range of books at each level helps teachers to match every child's needs, whether it is for more practice or for more challenge. Book band information on the book covers enables you to match the books to children's reading ability levels. Some children may benefit from reading some of the stories at a lower level than the guided reading text to build confidence and fluency. More confident fluent readers will enjoy the *All Stars*, *Robins* and *Jackdaws* books. *Robins* and *All Stars* have content suitable for the age group and have more variety in vocabulary and presentation. *Jackdaws* contain fiction and non-fiction, and are suitable for confident and slightly more mature readers.

Reading Skills

At each stage children will benefit from independent activities to support their skills development, they include the *Sequencing PCMs*, the *Games* boxes, *Group Activity Sheets* and the *Comprehension Photocopy Masters*. *Oxford Reading Tree Online*, and software such as *Talking Stories* and *Clicker* for Stages 1–5, provide electronic opportunities for consolidation and vocabulary enrichment.

Reading at home

You may choose to send the Oxford Reading Tree books home so that children can practise their reading skills with their parents and carers – guidance on this, and some useful bookmarks to photocopy, can be found on pages 102–103. There are also notes on the inside cover of the books themselves. In addition, Oxford Reading Tree *Read at Home* is a series of books which have been specially designed to be read at home, supporting the reading skills children are learning at school.

Using Oxford Reading Tree alongside other resources

Whether you are using Oxford Reading Tree as your main literacy resource at Key Stage 1, or as part of a mixture of resources, you will find that it fits very well alongside other books and literacy materials. As all of the Oxford Reading Tree books are book banded, you can see instantly how they align with other reading and literacy resources at similar levels. You will also find that the books work well alongside the best of children's literature from trade publishers. Many well-known and respected children's writers have contributed books to the *Snapdragons* and *All Stars* strands, including Julia Donaldson, Geraldine McCaughren and Martin Waddell.

Teaching English as an Additional Language using Oxford Reading Tree

As well as providing an ideal teaching resource for children whose first language is English, Oxford Reading Tree can also be used very successfully with children learning English as an Additional Language (EAL). The core characters and the situations they find themselves in are easy for most children to identify with, and the very gradual build-up of vocabulary and reading skills is helpful to EAL learners as well as to native speakers of English. The emphasis on speaking and listening within Oxford Reading Tree is also beneficial to EAL learners, as discussing and enjoying the stories together is a great way of encouraging talk in a fun and non-stressful context.

The Oxford Reading Tree *Teacher's Guide For Children Learning English* includes lessons and photocopiable pages to introduce and make best use of Oxford Reading Tree as a resource to teach English as a second language.

Case study

Jane Langrell, Literacy Co-ordinator at Canning Street Primary School, Newcastle, says:

"Ours is an inner-city primary school in the West End of Newcastle. About 75% of our children are learners of English as an additional language (EAL). We have a high proportion of children with special needs, too.

We find Oxford Reading Tree works really well for all the children, including the EAL learners. For the EAL children in particular, it's really important that Reading Tree gives so much support for speaking and listening as well as developing early reading skills.

We start off by introducing and talking about the characters and what they get up to, using the *Big Books* as a focus so that children can see what we're talking about. We also use the *Flash Cards* to introduce words and characters. One of the things we really like about Reading Tree is the repetition of phrases and key words, which helps to build up children's confidence. And as teachers we also feel confident that if children work through the early stages systematically, they will get to know a wide range of 'tricky' words as well as learning how to read decodable words.

The children really enjoy the humour in the stories, and they find it easy to relate to the characters so they really do want to read on and find out what happens to them. We use Oxford Reading Tree throughout the school, and particularly in Reception and Key Stage 1. Of course we use lots of other books and resources too, particularly with the older children, but in the first couple of years at school, Reading Tree really is at the heart of our children's reading."

The flexibility of Oxford Reading Tree

Oxford Reading Tree can be used in a very wide variety of classroom settings, and users often have their own favourite aspects of the programme. The following case studies show how three different schools use Oxford Reading Tree.

Case study

Philippa Roy-Chowdhury, Deputy Head Teacher and Literacy Co-ordinator at Thorley Hill Primary School, Bishop's Stortford, Hertfordshire, says:

"At Thorley Hill we have a one form entry and a total of 230 pupils, including the Nursery. We have a mixed catchment area, and are admitting a growing number of children with special needs, including Down's Syndrome and Autism. At present we have only a few children with English as an Additional Language, but this may well change as expansion at Stansted Airport attracts more workers from abroad.

We use Oxford Reading Tree books and materials extensively up to Year 4. Although we supplement it with other schemes, Oxford Reading Tree is our core programme for both guided reading and take-home books. I especially like the early stories as they motivate children to read. The stories are exciting but also offer support through repetition and careful progression to more demanding vocabulary. The staff feel confident with the scheme and also enjoy sharing the stories with the children.

Although the children gain confidence from familiarity with the style and the characters appearing in the books, I use other schemes and books to broaden their experience of other authors and writing styles.

We have just purchased Oxford Reading Tree *MagicPage* and I am about to use an INSET time to introduce it to all the staff. I am really excited about using it and think it will be a very useful tool for teachers as well as exciting for the children.

I have used Oxford Reading Tree since its introduction over twenty years ago. I think it is a really valuable scheme, especially the stories that can be linked to other subjects, such as the Victorians or the Egyptians. I have yet to find a child who doesn't enjoy the books!"

Case study

Rachel Crouch, Headteacher, St Nicholas' Primary School, Oxford, says:

"St Nicholas' is an inner city school with 340 pupils aged 3 to 11. Around a quarter have Special Educational Needs and just over a quarter have English as an Additional Language.

We find *Oxford Reading Tree* very useful throughout the school but also use it higher up the school for children with special educational and language needs. In the classroom we use the stories for guided reading. We also make good use of the *Big Books*, *Talking Stories* and CDs. The stories are bookbanded and children often choose them to read at home. Children are attracted to the excellent illustrations, and the familiar characters give them confidence when approaching a new story.

Teachers find that it is easy to link stories to other subject areas, e.g. *Roman Adventure* and *Viking Adventure*, and everyone appreciates the support provided by repetition and the pictures.

We find that the *eSongbirds* software supports our phonics programme very well, and the children who lack confidence love the *Talking Stories*. I would especially recommend the *Talking Stories* to other schools, especially for EAL and SEN children. It is wonderful to see them gain a sense of achievement from using this material."

Case study

Liz Mason, Reception teacher, Greave Primary School, Stockport, says:

"I have only been using *MagicPage* since Sept'07 but its impact on children's progress in literacy has been tremendous.

Oxford Reading Tree *MagicPage* has engaged all my Reception class children from the most able to those with limited literacy skills. Its Interactive Whiteboard format captivates the children's attention and there is a real sense of excitement and anticipation as they sit on the carpet. The software has not only supported my literacy teaching but impacted greatly on the children's competence in IT. The use of the video, recorded sound, teacher and navigation tools has given my class of 4 year olds a wealth of IT expertise whilst at the same time a genuine love of story like no other resource I've used. It is a joy to watch the children, retell stories about their favourite Oxford Reading Tree characters with such expression and enthusiasm, whilst confidently navigating through an electronic book to an audience. Oxford Reading Tree *MagicPage* has greatly improved the children's quality of story telling."

Oxford Reading Tree and the revised Northern Ireland Primary Curriculum

Oxford Reading Tree is fully in line with the requirements of the revised Northern Ireland Curriculum for Language and Literacy, providing children and teachers with many opportunities to cover the objectives for Talking and Listening, Reading and Writing.

The *Teaching Notes* for each individual book within Oxford Reading Tree show how each book relates to the Northern Ireland Curriculum. The information below summarises some of the key ways in which Oxford Reading Tree supports each of the key areas within Language and Literacy.

Talking and Listening

Foundation Stage (Year 1/P1 and Year 2/P2)

- Children's **attention and listening skills**, and **social use of language**, can be developed using Oxford Reading Tree *MagicPage*, *Big Books*, *Big Talkabout Cards*, *Talking Stories* and *Story CDs*.
- **Phonological awareness** can be developed using *Songbirds*, *eSongbirds* and *Floppy's Phonics*.
- **Language and thinking skills**, and **extended vocabulary**, can be supported using the whole range of Oxford Reading Tree resources at Stages 1–5.

Key Stage 1 (Year 3/P3 and Year 4/P4)

- Oxford Reading Tree *MagicPage*
- Oxford Reading Tree *Talking Stories* and *Oxford Reading Tree Online*

Reading

Foundation Stage

- *Songbirds* and *eSongbirds*
- Oxford Reading Tree *MagicPage*
- Biff, Chip and Kipper stories, *Big Books* and *Sequencing Cards Photocopy Masters*

Key Stage 1

- Oxford Reading Tree *MagicPage* and *Oxford Reading Tree Online*
- Biff, Chip and Kipper stories
- *Snapdragons*, *Fireflies* and *Glow-worms*
- *Comprehension Photocopy Masters*

Writing

Foundation Stage

- Oxford Reading Tree *MagicPage*
- *Extended Stories Photocopy Masters*
- *Routes to Writing*

Key Stage 1

- *Routes to Writing*
- Oxford Reading Tree *MagicPage*

Suggested teaching sequence flow chart

This flowchart shows you how all the Oxford Reading Tree components will help you teach the full range of literacy skills.

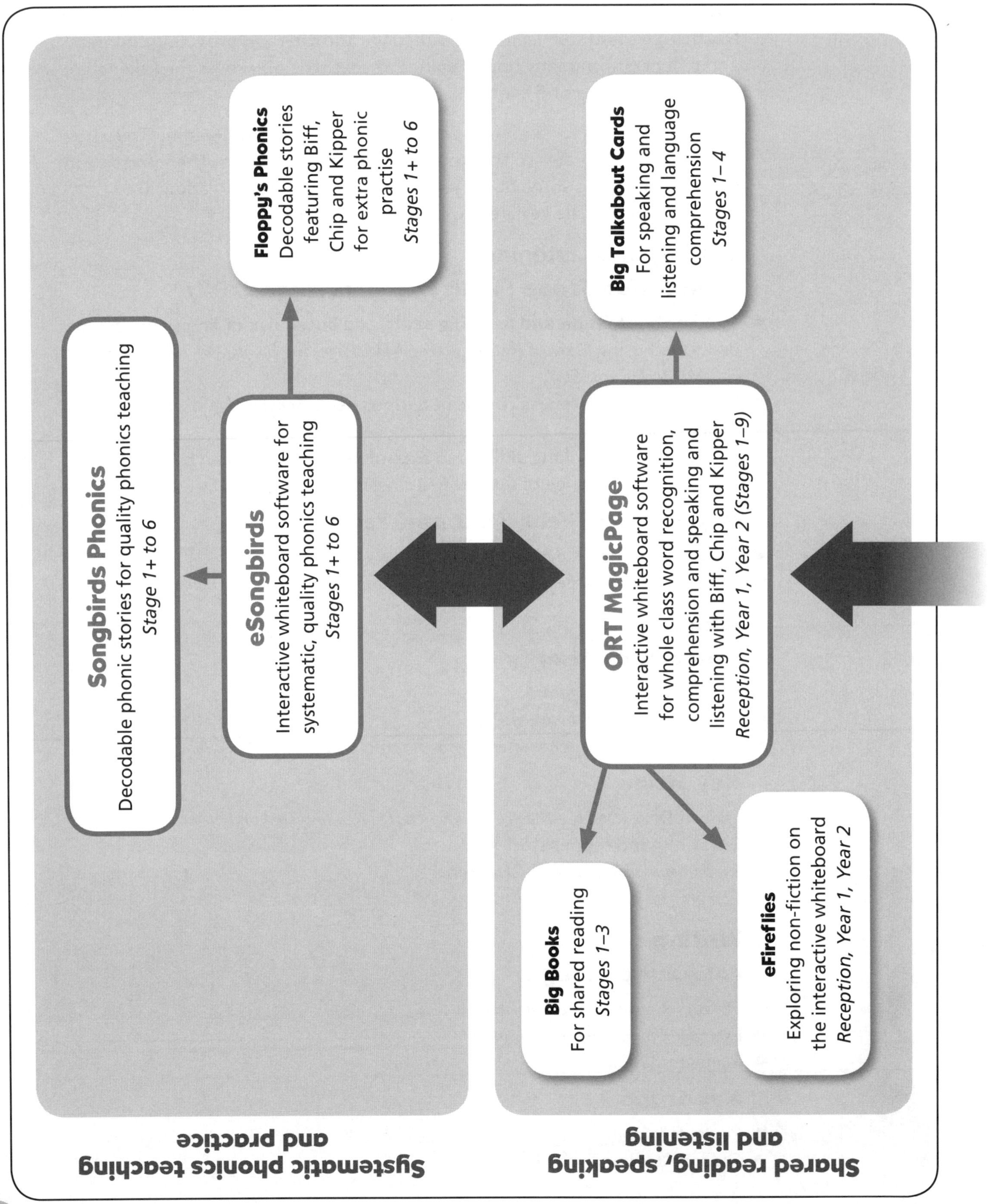

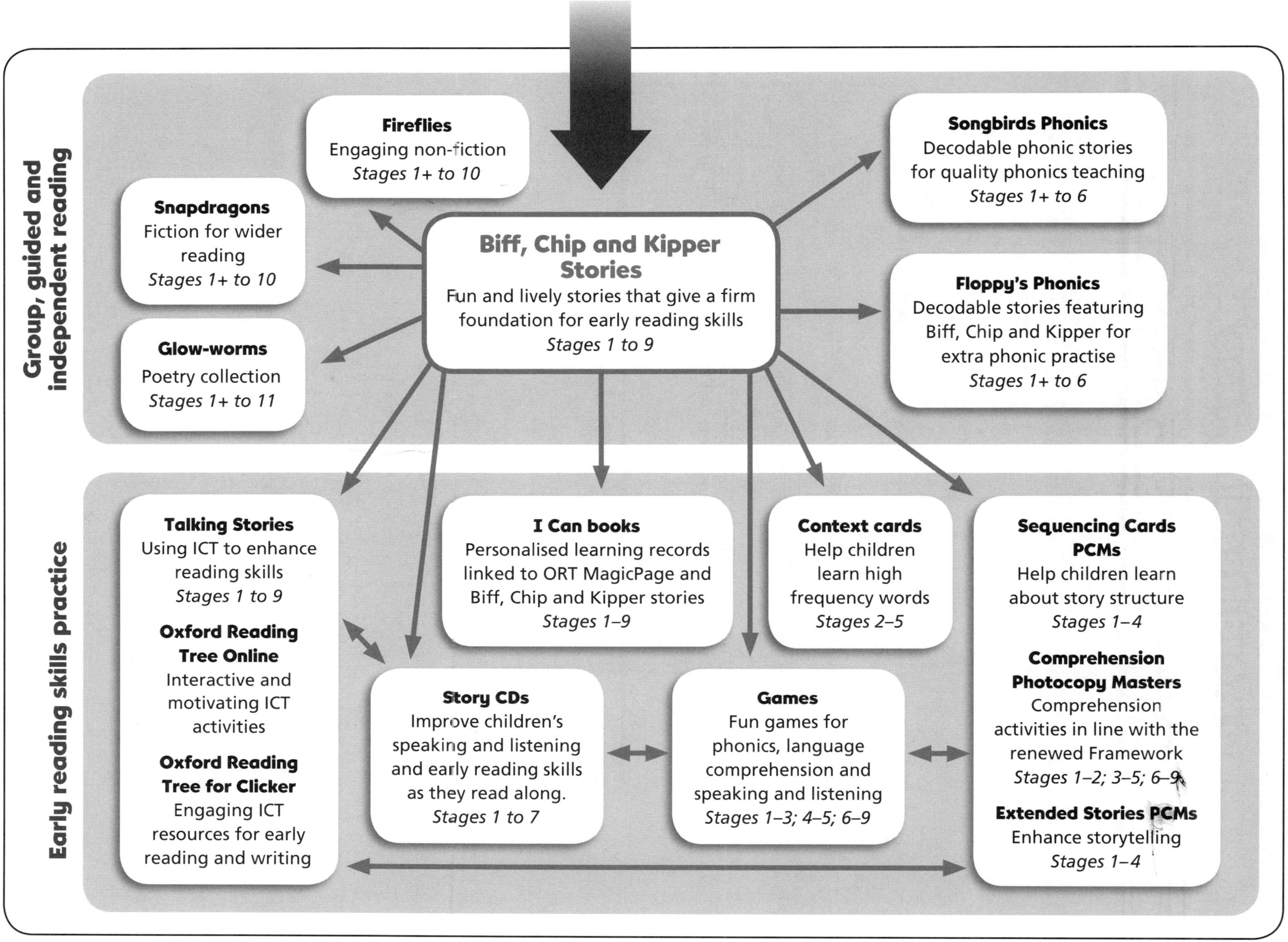
Group, guided and independent reading
Fireflies
Engaging non-fiction
Stages 1+ to 10
Snapdragons
Fiction for wider reading
Stages 1+ to 10
Glow-worms
Poetry collection
Stages 1+ to 11
Biff, Chip and Kipper Stories
Fun and lively stories that give a firm foundation for early reading skills
Stages 1 to 9
Songbirds Phonics
Decodable phonic stories for quality phonics teaching
Stages 1+ to 6
Floppy's Phonics
Decodable stories featuring Biff, Chip and Kipper for extra phonic practise
Stages 1+ to 6
Early reading skills practice
Talking Stories
Using ICT to enhance reading skills
Stages 1 to 9
Oxford Reading Tree Online
Interactive and motivating ICT activities
Oxford Reading Tree for Clicker
Engaging ICT resources for early reading and writing
I Can books
Personalised learning records linked to ORT MagicPage and Biff, Chip and Kipper stories
Stages 1–9
Context cards
Help children learn high frequency words
Stages 2–5
Sequencing Cards PCMs
Help children learn about story structure
Stages 1–4
Comprehension Photocopy Masters
Comprehension activities in line with the renewed Framework
Stages 1–2; 3–5; 6–9
Extended Stories PCMs
Enhance storytelling
Stages 1–4
Story CDs
Improve children's speaking and listening and early reading skills as they read along.
Stages 1 to 7
Games
Fun games for phonics, language comprehension and speaking and listening
Stages 1–3; 4–5; 6–9

Oxford Reading Tree

Sample lesson plans

The following lesson plans include:

- Guidance on how to teach phonics using Oxford Reading Tree.
- 1 lesson plan per stage to show how to teach reading and writing using Oxford Reading Tree. All the plans begin with ideas for speaking and listening.

Introduce and teach phonics with eSongbirds

Use one of the Oxford Reading Tree's phonic teaching programme CD-ROMs (*eSongbirds*) on your whiteboard.

- Choose a book and select the letter pattern you want to focus on.
- Click 'See animation' to demonstrate how the letter pattern matches the sound, and get children to practise saying and writing the sound in the air.
- Click on 'Activities' to practise using the phonics.
- Read the talking story with the class.
- Children can then use the CD-ROMs independently, reading the talking story, doing the activities and the electronic assessments.

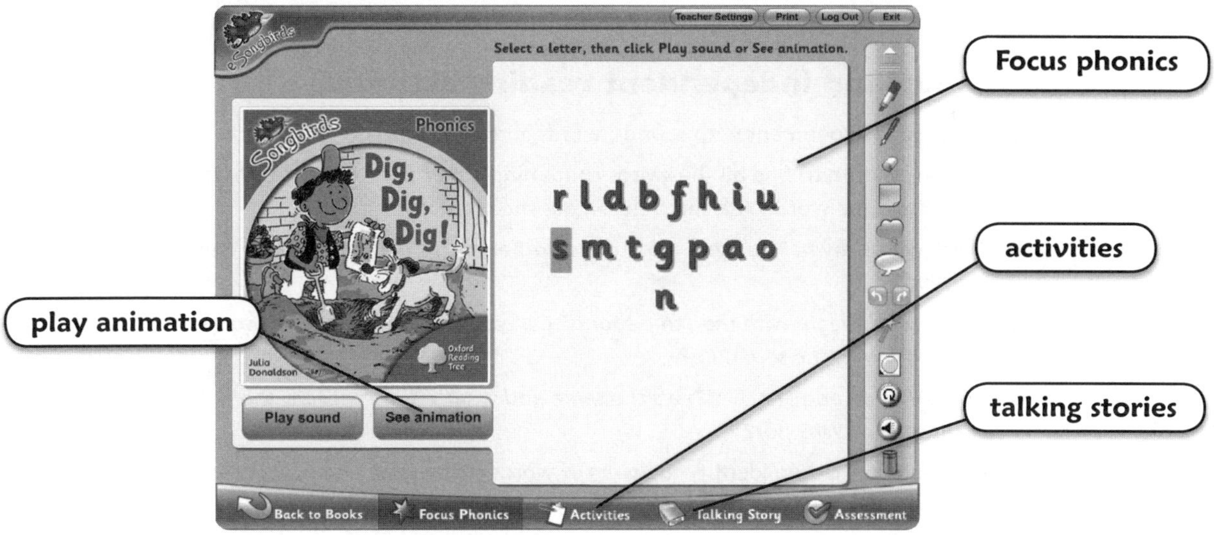

Use phonics to read a Songbirds book

- Remind children of the phonics you focused on in the whiteboard session by using the 'Introduce the phonics' section in the *Songbirds Teaching Notes*.
- Read the *Songbirds* book with a group of children, using the 'Group or guided reading' section in the *Songbirds Teaching Notes*.
- Remind the children to use the sounds of the letter patterns to sound out the words, and encourage them to read the book at their own pace within the group.
- Focus on each child's reading, and use the assessment points in the *Songbirds Teaching Notes* to assess decoding skills. See below.

Independent reading

(W) Encourage each of the children to read the whole book at his or her own pace, sounding out and blending words they do not recognise. Listen in to each child reading and provide lots of praise and support.

- Praise the children for sounding out and blending sounds to read words they do not recognise and for recognising familiar words.

Assessment Observe the children to check that they can:

- *(R, AF1)* match one spoken word to one written word
- *(R, AF1)* confidently give the sound for all the focus letter patterns

Practise phonics with a Floppy's Phonics book

- Remind the children of the focus phonics from your *Songbirds* sessions and get them to identify those letter patterns in a *Floppy's Phonics* book.
- Practise decoding skills by reading a *Floppy's Phonics* book in a group session, using the 'Group or guided reading' section in the *Floppy's Phonics Teaching Notes.*
- Focus on each child's reading, and use the assessment points in the *Floppy's Phonics Teaching Notes* to assess decoding and comprehension.
- Use the 'Group and independent reading activities' section in the *Floppy's Phonics Teaching Notes* to reinforce focus phonics and deepen comprehension. See below.

Group and independent reading activities

Objective Explore and experiment with sounds, words and letters (5.1).

W Ask the children to find all the words containing *a* on page 1 (*had, cat, hat*). Write the three words. Ask the children questions such as:

- *Which words rhyme? Can you think of any other words that rhyme with 'cat' and "hat"?*
- *Which words begin with the same sound? Can you think of any other words that begin with the sound /h/?*
- *Look at "had" and "hat". What's the same and what's different? Do the words rhyme? Why not?*

Assessment *(AF1)* Can the children identify the pairs of words that rhyme and the words that begin with the same sound?

Stage I Kipper Stories At School

Speaking and Listening

Use Oxford Reading Tree *MagicPage CD-ROM Stages 1–2* and accompanying *Teaching Guide* to introduce the story and talk about the main events (Kipper doesn't want to go to school on his first day, but then he has so much fun that he doesn't want to go home). Refer to the *MagicPage Teaching Guide* pages 16–17.

See Oxford Reading Tree *Teaching Notes* for further speaking and listening activities.

Shared Reading

Read the story using Oxford Reading Tree *MagicPage CD-ROM Stages 1–2* and talk about it with the children, or use the *Extended Stories Photocopy Masters* to help you tell the extended story and discuss it with the children. Then use the Oxford Reading Tree *Teaching Notes* to focus on word recognition (see below).

Objective Read some high frequency words (5.7).

Know that print carries meaning and, in English, is read from left to right (7.1).

Ⓦ Write this sentence on a board: 'Kipper is at school.' Ask the children to read the sentence aloud as you point to each word from left to right. Ask the children to substitute Kipper's name for the name of some of the children in the class.

Assessment *(R, AF1)* Do the children read the correct word as you point to it?

Group and Independent Reading

Read *At School* with a group using the accompanying *Teaching Notes*.

Assessment Check that children:

- *(R, AF2)* notice enough information in the pictures to tell and understand the story
- *(R, AF1)* open the book and 'read' it from left to right

Assess whether children can follow and understand the story. Check that they can open the book and turn the pages from left to right. Use ideas from the *Teaching Notes* pages 8-10 to practise early reading skills (see above).

Use Oxford Reading Tree *MagicPage I Can* book page 4 to assess children's understanding of the story and Kipper's feelings.

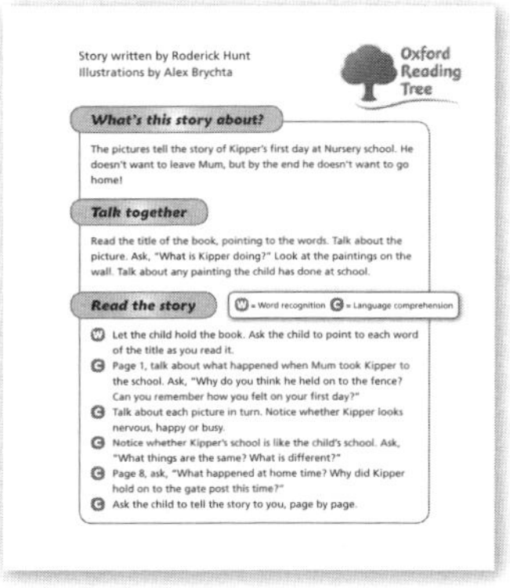

Story written by Roderick Hunt
Illustrations by Alex Brychta

Oxford Reading Tree

What's this story about?

The pictures tell the story of Kipper's first day at Nursery school. He doesn't want to leave Mum, but by the end he doesn't want to go home!

Talk together

Read the title of the book, pointing to the words. Talk about the picture. Ask, "What is Kipper doing?" Look at the paintings on the wall. Talk about any painting the child has done at school.

Read the story Ⓦ = Word recognition Ⓒ = Language comprehension

Ⓦ Let the child hold the book. Ask the child to point to each word of the title as you read it.
Ⓒ Page 1, talk about what happened when Mum took Kipper to the school. Ask, "Why do you think he held on to the fence? Can you remember how you felt on your first day?"
Ⓒ Talk about each picture in turn. Notice whether Kipper looks nervous, happy or busy.
Ⓒ Notice whether Kipper's school is like the child's school. Ask, "What things are the same? What is different?"
Ⓒ Page 8, ask, "What happened at home time? Why did Kipper hold on to the gate post this time?"
Ⓒ Ask the child to tell the story to you, page by page.

Reinforce by sending the book home, asking parents to use the inside cover notes.

Writing

Use the Oxford Reading Tree *MagicPage CD-ROM* 'Change' section to rewrite the story (refer to *MagicPage Teaching Guide*, page 22).

Stage 1+ First Sentences Reds and Blues

Speaking and Listening

Use the big book version of *Reds and Blues*. Turn to pages 20–21 of the Stage 1+ *Big Books Teaching Notes* to introduce the story and talk about the main events (Chip is on the red football team and Biff is on the blue team. They have an exciting game and everyone gets very muddy). Use the *Big Books Teaching Notes* pages 20–21 to read and talk about the extended story, and page 22 for other speaking and listening activities.

Shared Reading

Read the story using the *Big Book*, and use the suggested guided responses on page 21 of the *Big Books Teaching Notes*. Pages 22–23 of the *Big Books Teaching Notes* have suggestions for shared reading activities, including using phonic knowledge to decode words (see below).

Anticipating the text through guided responses

	Lead in	Guided responses
Page 1	*What does Chip say about his team?*	We are all in red.
Pages 2/3	*What does Biff say about her team?*	We are all in red.
Pages 4/5	*What do some of the grown-ups shout?* *What do the other grown-ups shout?*	Come on the reds! Come on the blues!
Pages 6/7	*What does Mum ask herself? What else does Mum ask?*	Who is in red? Who is in blue?
Page 8	*What does Chip say?*	We are all in muddy.

Group and Independent Reading

Read *Reds and Blues* with a group using the accompanying *Teaching Notes*.

Assessment Check that children:

- *(R, AF1)* start reading from left to right automatically
- *(R, AF1)* can read on sight the familiar high frequency words.

Assess children's phonic and comprehension knowledge (see above). Practise reading words with common digraphs using suggestions in the *Teaching Notes*, pages 20–21.

Make copies of the story using the Oxford Reading Tree *Sequencing Photocopy Masters* for each of the children to fold up and make their own book.

Reinforce by sending the book home, asking parents to use the inside cover notes.

Story written by Roderick Hunt
Illustrations by Alex Brychta

Oxford Reading Tree

What's this story about?

The children are playing football. There are two teams, but which is which at the end of the game?

Talk together

Read the title on the cover and talk about the teams. Ask, "Do you know the names of any of the characters? Do you like playing and watching team games?"

Read the story (W = Word recognition C = Language comprehension)

- W Begin to read the story together. If the child is keen to read alone, encourage him or her to do so.
- C Pages 1 and 2, talk about why the teams are in different colour shirts.
- W Page 1, point out the tricky word 'are' and say the word to the child. Repeat for 'come' on page 4 and 'who' on page 6.
- C Pages 6 and 7 ask, "Why are the players getting dirty? Do you think Biff scored a goal?"
- C Page 8 ask, "What do you think the score was at the end of the game?"
- W Encourage children to sound out the phonemes all through the word 'muddy'('m–u–dd–y').

Writing

Use the suggestions in the Stage 1+ *Big Books Teaching Notes* (page 23) and the Stage 1+ *First Sentences Teaching Notes* (page 23) to do related writing activities with the children.

Writing

Objective Write their own names and other things such as labels and captions and begin to form simple sentences sometimes using punctuation (11).
You will need strips of paper and reusable adhesive.

- C *(Summarising)* Look at the pictures and retell the story together in your own words.
- C *(Clarifying)* Go back to page 1 and ask: *What colour is Chip wearing?*
- Write 'Chip is in red' on a strip of paper and fix it to the book.
- On page 2 ask: *What colour is Biff wearing?*
- W As you write 'Biff is in blue' ask the children to tell you the first letter of each word.
- On page 8 ask: *Who is muddy?* Write the sentence, e.g. 'Everyone is muddy.' Ask for help on how to spell the words. Fix the sentence to the book.
- Read the new sentences as you reread the book together.

Assessment *(W, AF8)* Did the children make phonetically plausible attempts to spell words?

Stage 2 Stories The Toys' Party

Speaking and Listening

Use Oxford Reading Tree *MagicPage CD-ROM Stages 1–2* and accompanying *Teaching Guide* to introduce the story and talk about the main events (Kipper organises a party for his toys, bakes a cake and makes a mess). Refer to the *MagicPage Teaching Guide* pages 48–49.

See Oxford Reading Tree *Teaching Notes* for further speaking and listening activities.

Shared Reading

Read the story using Oxford Reading Tree *MagicPage CD-ROM Stages 1–2* and talk about it with the children. Discuss the story using the *Context Cards* and put them in order with the children. Then use the Oxford Reading Tree *Teaching Notes* to focus on word level work (see below).

Group and independent reading activities

Objective Link sounds and letters, naming and sounding letters (5.2). Read simple words by sounding out and blending from left to right (5.6).

W On page 8, ask children to help you read the word 'put'. Model segmenting into phonemes (sounding out in order) and blending them to read the word. On page 9, ask a child to show you how to read 'put' in the same way.

Group and Independent Reading

Read *The Toys' Party* with a group using the accompanying *Teaching Notes*.

Assessment Check that children:

- *(R, AF1)* track text matching letters to sounds
- *(R, AF1)* use phonic knowledge to sound out and blend the phonemes in words, particularly the phonic words (see chart on page 4).

Assess children's phonic and comprehension knowledge (see above). Practise reading decodable words using ideas from the *Teaching Notes* pages 8–9.

Make copies of the story using the Oxford Reading Tree *Sequencing Photocopy Masters* for each of the children to fold up and make their own book.

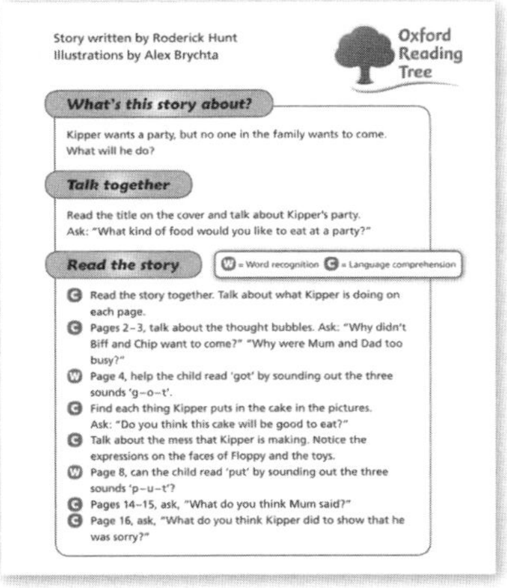

Story written by Roderick Hunt
Illustrations by Alex Brychta

Oxford Reading Tree

What's this story about?

Kipper wants a party, but no one in the family wants to come. What will he do?

Talk together

Read the title on the cover and talk about Kipper's party.
Ask: "What kind of food would you like to eat at a party?"

Read the story (W = Word recognition C = Language comprehension)

- C Read the story together. Talk about what Kipper is doing on each page.
- C Pages 2–3, talk about the thought bubbles. Ask: "Why didn't Biff and Chip want to come?" "Why were Mum and Dad too busy?"
- W Page 4, help the child read 'got' by sounding out the three sounds 'g–o–t'.
- C Find each thing Kipper puts in the cake in the pictures. Ask: "Do you think this cake will be good to eat?"
- C Talk about the mess that Kipper is making. Notice the expressions on the faces of Floppy and the toys.
- W Page 8, can the child read 'put' by sounding out the three sounds 'p–u–t'?
- C Pages 14–15, ask, "What do you think Mum said?"
- C Page 16, ask, "What do you think Kipper did to show that he was sorry?"

Use Oxford Reading Tree *MagicPage I Can* book page 14 to assess children's understanding of sequence.

Reinforce by sending home, asking parents to use the inside cover notes.

Writing

Use the Oxford Reading Tree *MagicPage CD-ROM* 'Change' section to rewrite the story (refer to *MagicPage Teaching Guide*, page 54).

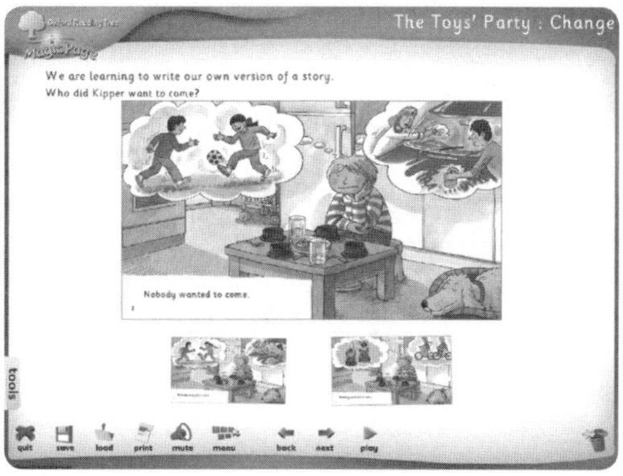

Stage 3 Stories The Rope Swing

Speaking and Listening

Use the big book version of *The Rope Swing*. Turn to pages 24–25 of the Stage 3 *Big Books Teaching Notes* to introduce the story and talk about the main events. (The children go on a rope swing. Floppy notices the rope is fraying. It looks as if the swing will break, but it doesn't – until the end, when it falls on Floppy's head!). Use the *Big Books Teaching Notes* pages 24–25 to read and talk about the extended story, and page 26 for other speaking and listening activities.

Shared Reading

Read the story using the *Big Book*, and use the suggested guided responses on page 25 of the *Big Books Teaching Notes* (see below). Pages 26–27 of the *Big Books Teaching Notes* have suggestions for shared reading activities, including recalling and talking about the story.

Anticipating the text through guided responses

	Lead in	Guided responses
Page 1	*Where did the children go?*	The children went to the stream.
Pages 2/3	(Point to the swing.) *What did they look at?* *Where did Wilf climb?*	They looked at the swing. Wilf climbed on the swing.
Pages 4/5	*Who pushed Wilf?* *What did Floppy look at?*	Chip pushed Wilf. Floppy looked at the rope.

Group and Independent Reading

Read *The Rope Swing* with a group using the accompanying *Teaching Notes*.

Assessment Check that children:

- *(R, AF1)* use a range of strategies to work out new words
- *(R, AF1)* recognise common inflections in spelling.

Assess children's phonic and comprehension knowledge (see above). Practise using phonic skills to decode words – see suggestions in the *Teaching Notes*, pages 24–25.

Make copies of the story using the Oxford Reading Tree *Sequencing Photocopy Masters* for each of the children to fold up and make their own book.

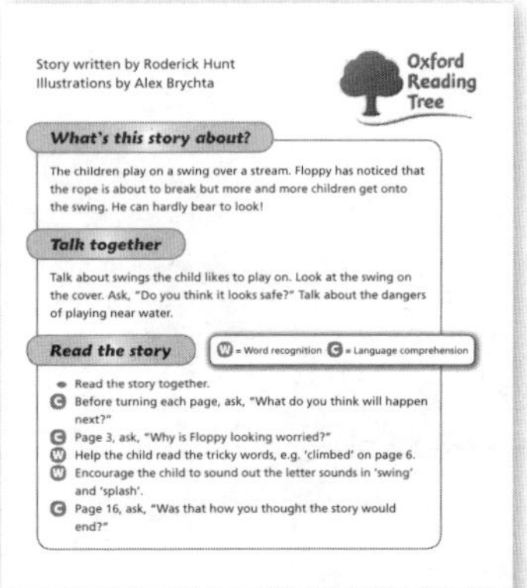

Story written by Roderick Hunt
Illustrations by Alex Brychta

Oxford Reading Tree

What's this story about?

The children play on a swing over a stream. Floppy has noticed that the rope is about to break but more and more children get onto the swing. He can hardly bear to look!

Talk together

Talk about swings the child likes to play on. Look at the swing on the cover. Ask, "Do you think it looks safe?" Talk about the dangers of playing near water.

Read the story (W = Word recognition, C = Language comprehension)

- Read the story together.
- (C) Before turning each page, ask, "What do you think will happen next?"
- (C) Page 3, ask, "Why is Floppy looking worried?"
- (W) Help the child read the tricky words, e.g. 'climbed' on page 6.
- (W) Encourage the child to sound out the letter sounds in 'swing' and 'splash'.
- (C) Page 16, ask, "Was that how you thought the story would end?"

Reinforce by sending the book home, asking parents to use the inside cover notes.

Writing

Use the suggestions in the Stage 3 *Big Books Teaching Notes* (page 27) and the *Teaching Notes* (page 27) to do related writing activities with the children.

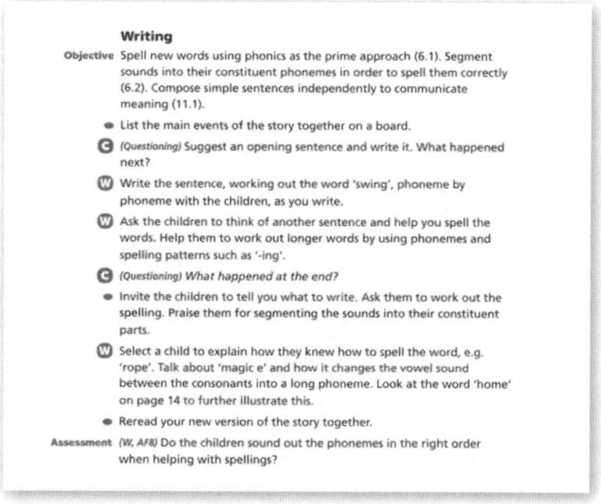

Writing

Objective Spell new words using phonics as the prime approach (6.1). Segment sounds into their constituent phonemes in order to spell them correctly (6.2). Compose simple sentences independently to communicate meaning (11.1).

- List the main events of the story together on a board.
- (C) *(Questioning)* Suggest an opening sentence and write it. What happened next?
- (W) Write the sentence, working out the word 'swing', phoneme by phoneme with the children, as you write.
- (W) Ask the children to think of another sentence and help you spell the words. Help them to work out longer words by using phonemes and spelling patterns such as '-ing'.
- (C) *(Questioning) What happened at the end?*
- Invite the children to tell you what to write. Ask them to work out the spelling. Praise them for segmenting the sounds into their constituent parts.
- (W) Select a child to explain how they knew how to spell the word, e.g. 'rope'. Talk about 'magic e' and how it changes the vowel sound between the consonants into a long phoneme. Look at the word 'home' on page 14 to further illustrate this.
- Reread your new version of the story together.

Assessment *(W, AF8)* Do the children sound out the phonemes in the right order when helping with spellings?

Stage 4 More Stories B Everyone Got Wet

Speaking and Listening

Use Oxford Reading Tree *MagicPage CD-ROM Stages 3–5* and accompanying *Teaching Guide* (pages 45–46) to introduce the story and talk about the main events. (The family are in the garden. Mum and Dad have to mend holes in the water butt and the hose, and they both get wet - twice. Then the hose bursts again, and this time the children get wet!). See Oxford Reading Tree Stage 4 *More Stories B Teaching Notes* page 31 for further speaking and listening activities.

Shared Reading

Read the story using Oxford Reading Tree *MagicPage CD-ROM Stages 3–5* and talk about it with the children, or use the *Extended Stories Photocopy Masters* to help you tell the extended story and discuss it with the children. Then use the Oxford Reading Tree Stage 4 *More Stories B Teaching Notes* pages 28–29 to focus on word recognition and understanding the story (see below).

Returning to the text

C *(Questioning, Clarifying)* Check their understanding and clarify any misunderstanding by asking a variety of questions that require recall, inference and deduction such as: *What did Dad say when he had mended the water butt?* (page 4) *Why did Dad put the new water butt on the bricks?* (page 12) *How do you think Mum felt when she got wet again?* (page 19)

Group and Independent Reading

Read *Everyone Got Wet* with a group using the accompanying *Teaching Notes.*

Assessment Check that children:

- *(R, AF1)* track text matching letters to sounds
- *(R, AF1)* use phonic knowledge to sound out and blend the phonemes in words, particularly the decodable words (see chart on page 4).

Assess whether children can match letters to sounds as they read, and use their phonic knowledge to read decodable words (see above). Use ideas from the *Teaching Notes* pages 29-30 to practise reading skills.

Use Oxford Reading Tree *MagicPage I Can* book page 12 to assess children's understanding of the story and the characters' feelings.

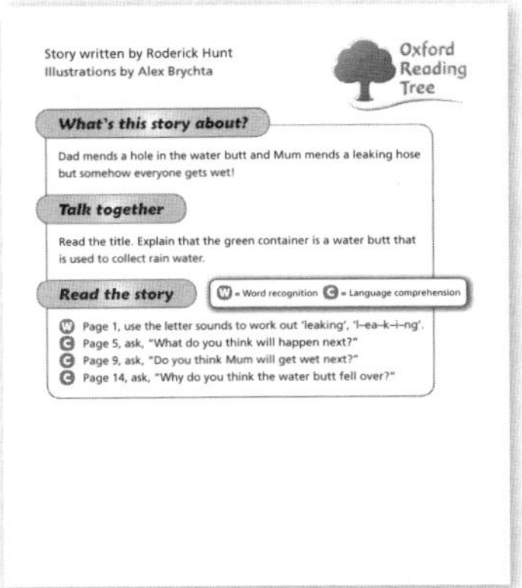

Story written by Roderick Hunt
Illustrations by Alex Brychta

Oxford Reading Tree

What's this story about?

Dad mends a hole in the water butt and Mum mends a leaking hose but somehow everyone gets wet!

Talk together

Read the title. Explain that the green container is a water butt that is used to collect rain water.

Read the story (W = Word recognition, C = Language comprehension)

W Page 1, use the letter sounds to work out 'leaking', 'l–ea–k–i–ng'.
C Page 5, ask, "What do you think will happen next?"
C Page 9, ask, "Do you think Mum will get wet next?"
C Page 14, ask, "Why do you think the water butt fell over?"

Reinforce by sending the book home, asking parents to use the inside cover notes.

Writing

Use the Oxford Reading Tree *MagicPage CD-ROM* 'Change' section to rewrite the story (refer to *MagicPage Teaching Guide*, pages 54–55).

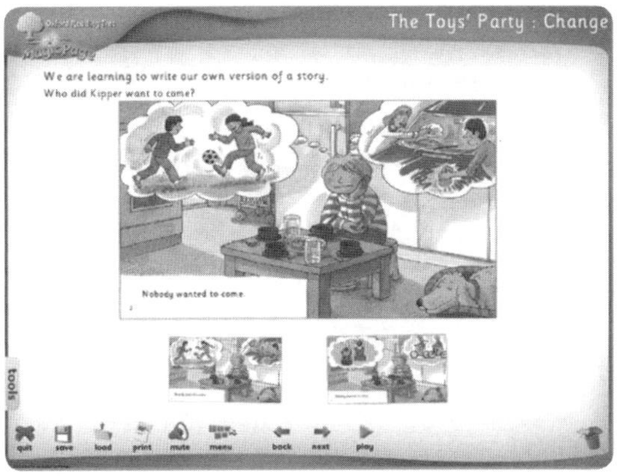

Stage 5 Stories Pirate Adventure

Speaking and Listening

Use Oxford Reading Tree *MagicPage CD-ROM Stages 3–5* and accompanying *Teaching Guide* (pages 57–58) to introduce the story and talk about the main events. (The magic key takes the children to a beautiful tropical beach where they meet some pirates. At first they are scared, but the pirates only want the children to come to a party!). See Oxford Reading Tree Stage 5 *Teaching Notes* page 15 for further speaking and listening activities.

Shared Reading

Read the story using Oxford Reading Tree *MagicPage CD-ROM Stages 3–5* and talk about it with the children. Then use the Oxford Reading Tree Stage 5 *Teaching Notes* pages 12–13 to focus on phonic skills and understanding of the story (see below).

Returning to the text

C *(Questioning, Clarifying, Summarising)* Ask: *What are the most important events in this story? Why do you think Wilf and Wilma felt differently from Biff and Chip at the beginning of the story? Did their feelings change later?*

Group and Independent Reading

Read *Pirate Adventure* with a group using the accompanying *Teaching Notes*.

Assessment Check that children:

- *(R, AF1)* use their phonic knowledge and the context to read unfamiliar words such as 'frightened'
- *(R, AF2)* use comprehension skills to understand the events of the story.

Assess whether children can use their phonic skills and knowledge of the context to read less familiar words (see above). Use ideas from the *Teaching Notes* pages 13–14 to practise reading skills.

Use Oxford Reading Tree *MagicPage I Can* book page 12 to assess children's ability to write sentences about the story.

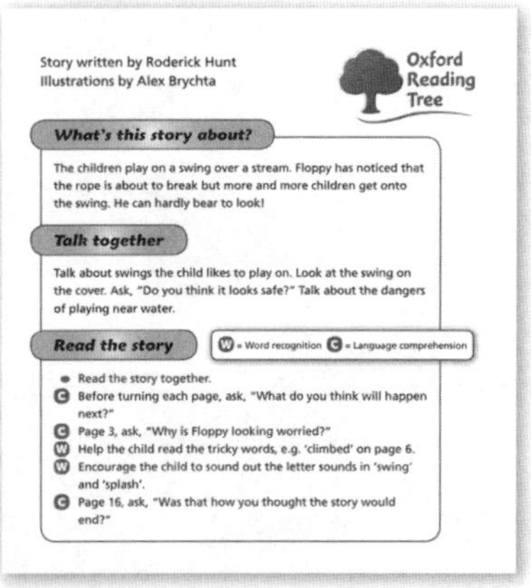
Story written by Roderick Hunt
Illustrations by Alex Brychta

Oxford Reading Tree

What's this story about?

The children play on a swing over a stream. Floppy has noticed that the rope is about to break but more and more children get onto the swing. He can hardly bear to look!

Talk together

Talk about swings the child likes to play on. Look at the swing on the cover. Ask, "Do you think it looks safe?" Talk about the dangers of playing near water.

Read the story W = Word recognition C = Language comprehension

- Read the story together.
- C Before turning each page, ask, "What do you think will happen next?"
- C Page 3, ask, "Why is Floppy looking worried?"
- W Help the child read the tricky words, e.g. 'climbed' on page 6.
- W Encourage the child to sound out the letter sounds in 'swing' and 'splash'.
- C Page 16, ask, "Was that how you thought the story would end?"

Reinforce by sending the book home, asking parents to use the inside cover notes.

Writing

Use the Oxford Reading Tree *MagicPage CD-ROM* 'Change' section to rewrite the story (refer to *MagicPage Teaching Guide*, pages 66–67).

Stage 6 Stories Land of the Dinosaurs

Speaking and Listening

Use Oxford Reading Tree *MagicPage CD-ROM Stages 6–9* and accompanying *Teaching Guide* to introduce the story and talk about the main events. (The magic takes the children back in time, they meet harmless and dangerous dinosaurs, Biff takes photographs to record their adventure, but is there a film in the camera?). Refer to the *MagicPage Teaching Guide* pages 18–19.

See Oxford Reading Tree *Teaching Notes* (pages 22–23) for further speaking and listening activities.

Shared Reading

Read the story using Oxford Reading Tree *MagicPage CD-ROM Stages 6–9* and talk about it with the children. Use the Oxford Reading Tree *Teaching Notes* (pages 20–21) 'Returning to the text' for comprehension questions and word activities (see below).

Returning to the text

C *(Summarising)* Ask the children to describe the creature the children met first. *What did they meet next? Which one was after that? Which was the last dinosaur they met? Why didn't they see any more?* Retell the sequence together using 'first', 'next', 'then' and 'after that'.

W On page 7, find 'egg' and 'eggs'. Ask: *What is the difference in the spelling? What is the difference in the meaning?* Ask children to find other examples of words in the book where an 's' has been added to make it plural (dinosaurs, photographs).

Group and Independent Reading

Read *Land of the Dinosaurs* with a group using the accompanying *Teaching Notes.*

Assessment Check that children:

- *(R, AF1)* read high frequency words with fluency and confidence
- *(R, AF4)* take account of the grammar and punctuation while reading aloud
- *(R, AF4)* are able to use the sense and structure of the sentence to decipher new words.

Assess children's phonic and comprehension knowledge (see above). Practise reading words with double consonants using ideas from the *Teaching Notes* page 22.

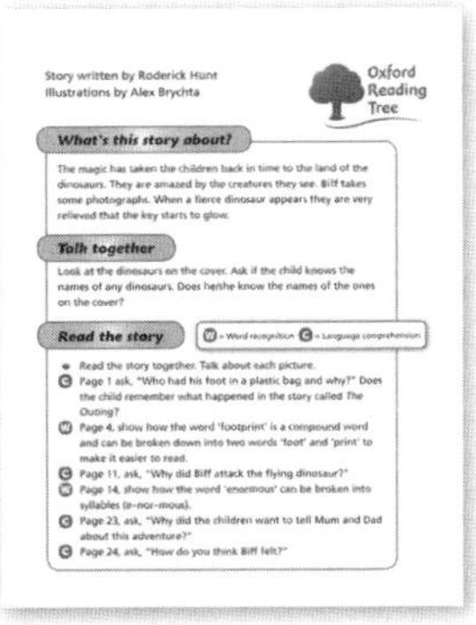
Story written by Roderick Hunt
Illustrations by Alex Brychta

Oxford Reading Tree

What's this story about?

The magic has taken the children back in time to the land of the dinosaurs. They are amazed by the creatures they see. Biff takes some photographs. When a fierce dinosaur appears they are very relieved that the key starts to glow.

Talk together

Look at the dinosaurs on the cover. Ask if the child knows the names of any dinosaurs. Does he/she know the names of the ones on the cover?

Read the story

W = Word recognition C = Language comprehension

- Read the story together. Talk about each picture.
- C Page 1 ask, "Who had his foot in a plastic bag and why?" Does the child remember what happened in the story called *The Outing?*
- W Page 4, show how the word 'footprint' is a compound word and can be broken down into two words 'foot' and 'print' to make it easier to read.
- C Page 11, ask, "Why did Biff attack the flying dinosaur?"
- W Page 14, show how the word 'enormous' can be broken into syllables (e-nor-mous).
- C Page 23, ask, "Why did the children want to tell Mum and Dad about this adventure?"
- C Page 24, ask, "How do you think Biff felt?"

Use Oxford Reading Tree *Magic Page I Can* book page 2 to assess children's ability to find key information in a text.

Reinforce by sending home, asking parents to use the inside cover notes.

Writing

Use the Oxford Reading Tree *MagicPage CD-ROM* 'Change' section for ideas to change and rewrite the story (refer to *MagicPage Teaching Guide*, page 27).

Stage 7 Stories Lost in the Jungle

Speaking and Listening

Use Oxford Reading Tree *MagicPage CD-ROM Stages 6–9* and accompanying *Teaching Guide* to introduce the story and talk about the main events (Mum is given tropical plants for her birthday; the magic takes the children to the jungle where they meet two explorers; they find a lost city). Refer to the *MagicPage Teaching Guide* pages 42–43.

See Oxford Reading Tree *Teaching Notes* (pages 38–39) for further speaking and listening activities.

Shared Reading

Read the story using Oxford Reading Tree *MagicPage CD-ROM Stages 6–9* and talk about it with the children. Use the Oxford Reading Tree *Teaching Notes* (pages 36–37) 'Returning to the text' for comprehension questions and word activities (see below).

C *(Clarifying)* Talk about the different settings in the story. Ask: *Which setting makes a better place to have an adventure?*

W Read page 9. Point out the statement, 'That monkey looks cross.' *Ask: Why doesn't Kipper say 'That monkey looked cross'?* Discuss how one is in the present and one is in the past.

Group and Independent Reading

Read *Lost in the Jungle* with a group using the accompanying *Teaching Notes*.

Assessment *(R, AF6)* Are the children able to write the irregular past tense verbs 'came', 'took', 'saw', 'ran' and 'fell'?

Assess children's phonic and comprehension knowledge (see above). Practise reading compound words using ideas from the *Teaching Notes* page 38.

Use Oxford Reading Tree *Magic Page I Can* book page 8 to assess children's ability to use descriptive language.

Reinforce by sending home, asking parents to use the inside cover notes.

Writing

Use the Oxford Reading Tree *MagicPage CD-ROM* 'Change' section to make changes to the story (refer to *MagicPage Teaching Guide*, page 53).

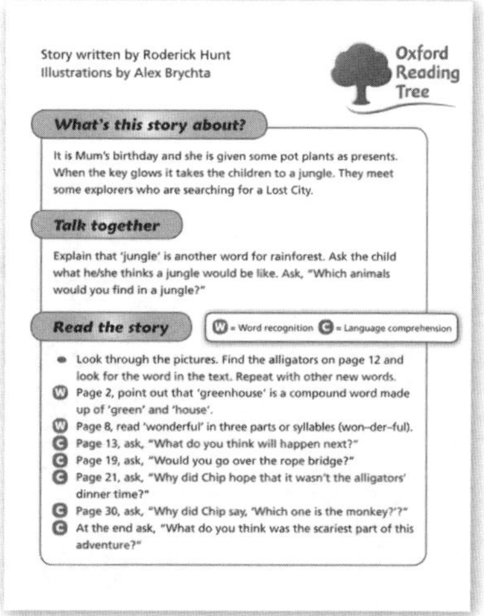
Story written by Roderick Hunt
Illustrations by Alex Brychta

Oxford Reading Tree

What's this story about?

It is Mum's birthday and she is given some pot plants as presents. When the key glows it takes the children to a jungle. They meet some explorers who are searching for a Lost City.

Talk together

Explain that 'jungle' is another word for rainforest. Ask the child what he/she thinks a jungle would be like. Ask, "Which animals would you find in a jungle?"

Read the story W = Word recognition C = Language comprehension

- Look through the pictures. Find the alligators on page 12 and look for the word in the text. Repeat with other new words.
- W Page 2, point out that 'greenhouse' is a compound word made up of 'green' and 'house'.
- W Page 8, read 'wonderful' in three parts or syllables (won-der-ful).
- C Page 13, ask, "What do you think will happen next?"
- C Page 19, ask, "Would you go over the rope bridge?"
- C Page 21, ask, "Why did Chip hope that it wasn't the alligators' dinner time?"
- C Page 30, ask, "Why did Chip say, 'Which one is the monkey?'?"
- C At the end ask, "What do you think was the scariest part of this adventure?"

Stage 8 Stories Victorian Adventure

Speaking and Listening

Use Oxford Reading Tree *MagicPage CD-ROM Stages 6–9* and accompanying *Teaching Guide* to introduce the story and talk about the main events (The magic takes the children to Victorian London; they meet Vicky, who takes them to play in Buckingham Palace; they meet Queen Victoria and, surprisingly, Gran). Refer to the *MagicPage Teaching Guide* pages 69-70.

See Oxford Reading Tree *Teaching Notes* pages 30–31 for further speaking and listening activities.

Shared Reading

Read the story using Oxford Reading Tree *MagicPage CD-ROM Stages 6–9* and talk about it with the children. Use the Oxford Reading Tree *Teaching Notes* 'Returning to the text' (page 29) to focus on the children's comprehension of the story (see below).

Returning to the text

- C *(Questioning)* On page 6, ask: *How does the text on this page tell us the time when the story was set?*
- C *(Questioning)* On page 13, ask: *How did Biff know where they were? Does this mean that the palace has changed or stayed the same?*

Group and Independent Reading

Read *Victorian Adventure* with a group using the accompanying *Teaching Notes*.

Assessment *(R, AF2)* Were the children able to use main points from the stories to make comparisons? Did they give reasons for their opinions?

Assess children's phonic and comprehension knowledge (see above). Practise spelling words with one, two three or four syllables using ideas from the *Teaching Notes* page 30.

Use Oxford Reading Tree *MagicPage I Can* book page 15 to assess children's ability to spell tricky parts of words.

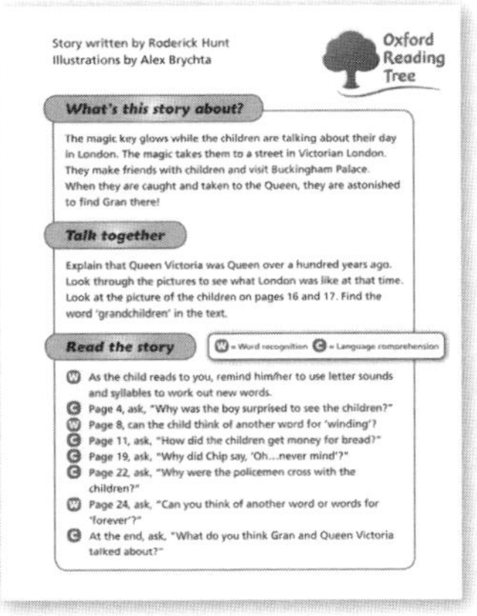

Story written by Roderick Hunt
Illustrations by Alex Brychta

Oxford Reading Tree

What's this story about?

The magic key glows while the children are talking about their day in London. The magic takes them to a street in Victorian London. They make friends with children and visit Buckingham Palace. When they are caught and taken to the Queen, they are astonished to find Gran there!

Talk together

Explain that Queen Victoria was Queen over a hundred years ago. Look through the pictures to see what London was like at that time. Look at the picture of the children on pages 16 and 17. Find the word 'grandchildren' in the text.

Read the story W = Word recognition C = Language comprehension

- W As the child reads to you, remind him/her to use letter sounds and syllables to work out new words.
- C Page 4, ask, "Why was the boy surprised to see the children?"
- W Page 8, can the child think of another word for 'winding'?
- C Page 11, ask, "How did the children get money for bread?"
- C Page 19, ask, "Why did Chip say, 'Oh…never mind'?"
- C Page 22, ask, "Why were the policemen cross with the children?"
- W Page 24, ask, "Can you think of another word or words for 'forever'?"
- C At the end, ask, "What do you think Gran and Queen Victoria talked about?"

Reinforce by sending home, asking parents to use the inside cover notes.

Writing

Use the Oxford Reading Tree *MagicPage CD-ROM* 'Change' section to make changes and rewrite the story (refer to *MagicPage Teaching Guide*, page 80).

Stage 9 Stories Storm Castle

Speaking and Listening

Use Oxford Reading Tree *MagicPage CD-ROM Stages 6–9* and accompanying *Teaching Guide* to introduce the story and talk about the main events (The magic takes the children inside a computer game; they solve problems to travel through the castle, and finally meet a giant robot operated by Nadim). Refer to the *MagicPage Teaching Guide* pages 83-84.

See Oxford Reading Tree *Teaching Notes* (page 15) for further speaking and listening activities.

Shared Reading

Read the story using Oxford Reading Tree *MagicPage CD-ROM Stages 6–9* and talk about it with the children. Use the Oxford Reading Tree *Teaching Notes* (page 13) 'Returning to the text' to focus on comprehension and word level work (see below).

- **W** On page 17, ask children to find two words that have different spellings of the phoneme 'ee' ('three' and 'key').
- **C** *(Clarifying)* Turn to page 20. Ask: *Show me how you think Kipper said 'that's funny'. Show me a different way of saying it.*

Group and Independent Reading

Read *Storm Castle* with a group using the accompanying *Teaching Notes.*

Assessment *(R, AF3)* Do children form a clearer picture of the role their character plays in the story's plot?

Assess children's phonic and comprehension knowledge (see above). Practise reading words with the phoneme 'ay' using ideas from the *Teaching Notes* page 14 .

Use Oxford Reading Tree *Magic Page I Can* book page 17 to assess children's ability to describe story settings.

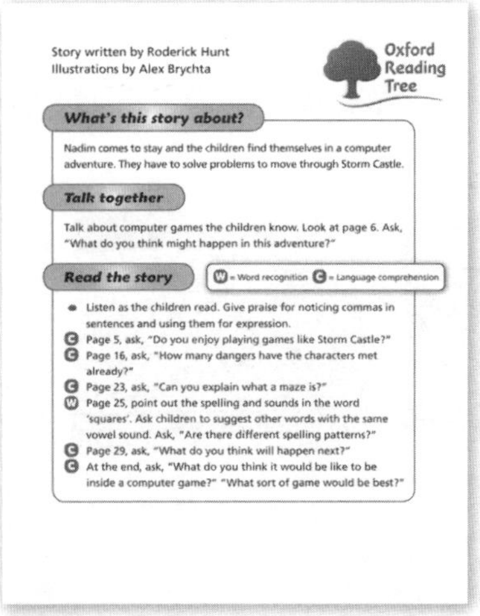

Story written by Roderick Hunt
Illustrations by Alex Brychta

Oxford Reading Tree

What's this story about?

Nadim comes to stay and the children find themselves in a computer adventure. They have to solve problems to move through Storm Castle.

Talk together

Talk about computer games the children know. Look at page 6. Ask, "What do you think might happen in this adventure?"

Read the story (W = Word recognition C = Language comprehension)

- Listen as the children read. Give praise for noticing commas in sentences and using them for expression.
- C Page 5, ask, "Do you enjoy playing games like Storm Castle?"
- C Page 16, ask, "How many dangers have the characters met already?"
- C Page 23, ask, "Can you explain what a maze is?"
- W Page 25, point out the spelling and sounds in the word 'squares'. Ask children to suggest other words with the same vowel sound. Ask, "Are there different spelling patterns?"
- C Page 29, ask, "What do you think will happen next?"
- C At the end, ask, "What do you think it would be like to be inside a computer game?" "What sort of game would be best?"

Reinforce by sending home, asking parents to use the inside cover notes.

Writing

Use the Oxford Reading Tree *MagicPage CD-ROM* 'Change' section to write a new description of a place, a monster or a robot, refer to *MagicPage Teaching Guide*, page 94.

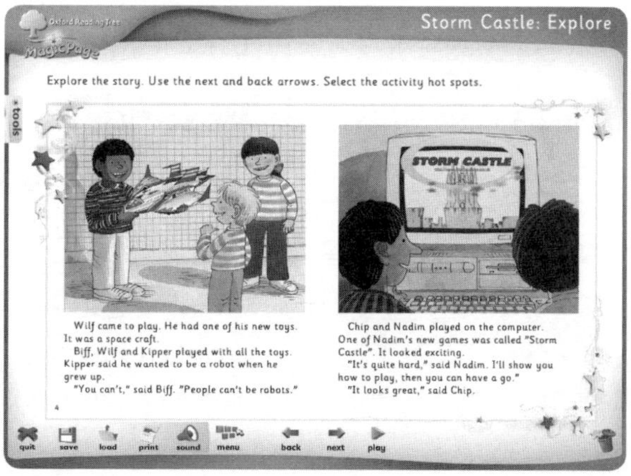

Oxford Reading Tree

Stage by stage planning charts

The following pages contain useful stage by stage charts to help you, plan, record and assess. For every stage there are:

- **Book recording charts** that allow you to record the books that each child or group has read. They contain useful information such as a selection of tricky and decodable words from the stories, National curriculum levels and book bands.

- **Checklists of reading skills** that allow you to record children's progress against objectives taken from the Primary National Strategy *Literacy Framework* and the *DCSF Standards Site Phonics Tracker.*

- **Lists of resources** to show which elements of Oxford Reading Tree are most useful to:

  Teach reading at each stage

  Consolidate and practise what has been learnt at each stage.

  For further reading and extension.

Key:

D = Decodable

T = Tricky

N = North

S = South (some words are tricky for longer depending on accent)

Stage 1 and 1+ book recording chart

You can use this chart to record books as children read them. It also shows the key information on each book at a glance.

Group name/children's initials ....

Biff, Chip and Kipper stories

	Title	Date read	Main high frequency words (D = Decodable , T = Tricky)	NC level	Bookband level
St 1 Kipper Stories	At School		**D**: at; **T**: school [Wordless stories]	Towards 1	Pink
	The Lost Teddy		**T**: the lost teddy [Wordless stories]	Towards 1	Pink
	The Library		**T**: the library [Wordless stories]	Towards 1	Pink
	The Haircut		**T**: the haircut [Wordless stories]	Towards 1	Pink
	Look Out!		**T**: look out [Wordless stories]	Towards 1	Pink
	Getting Up		**D**: up; **T**: getting [Wordless stories]	Towards 1	Pink
St 1 Biff and Chip Stories	The Apple		**T**: the apple [Wordless stories]	Towards 1	Pink
	The Big Box		**D**: big box; **T**: the [Wordless stories]	Towards 1	Pink
	Fetch!		**T**: fetch [Wordless stories]	Towards 1	Pink
	The Hedgehog		**T**: the hedgehog [Wordless stories]	Towards 1	Pink
	The Street Fair		**T**: the street fair [Wordless stories]	Towards 1	Pink
	The Swing Ball		**T**: the swing ball [Wordless stories]	Towards 1	Pink
St 1 First Words	A Good Trick		**D**: big box; **T**: little a	Towards 1	Pink
	Floppy Floppy		**T**: oh no	Towards 1	Pink
	Fun at the Beach		**D**: Dad Mum; **T**: oh and	Towards 1	Pink
	Six in a Bed		**D**: Dad Mum in; **T**: a and	Towards 1	Pink
	The Pancake		**D**: pan; **T**: the	Towards 1	Pink
	Who Is It?		**D**: Dad is it Mum ; **T**: no who a and	Towards 1	Pink
St 1 More First Words	Is It?		**D**: it yes; **T**: is	Towards 1	Pink
	Get On		**D**: get got on; **T**: oh no	Towards 1	Pink
	Floppy Did This		**D**: did it is Mum; **T**: oh no this	Towards 1	Pink
	Get Dad		**D**: Dad get Mum on; **T**: go	Towards 1	Pink
	Up You Go		**D**: Dad up; **T**: go no you	Towards 1	Pink
	I See		**D**: Dad Mum; **T**: I me we and see	Towards 1	Pink

Group name/children's initials ....

Biff, Chip and Kipper stories *continued*

	Title	Date read	Main high frequency words (D = Decodable , T = Tricky)	NC level	Bookband level
St1+ Patterned Stories	Fancy Dress		**D**: an Dad Mum; **T**: everyone happy was a	Towards 1	Pink
	The Headache		**D**: Dad had Mum; **T**: a	Towards 1	Pink
	The Pet Shop		**D**: pet rat; **T**: everyone oh no said shop the wanted a	Towards 1	Pink
	At the Park		**D**: at Mum on; **T**: everyone to the park went	Towards 1	Red
	Good Old Mum		**D**: big Mum on red; **T**: said a put	Towards 1	Red
	Push!		**D**: Mum it; **T**: car no pulled oh the was	Towards 1	Red
St 1+ More Patterned Stories	Making Faces		**D**: Dad Mum sad; **T**: good was	Towards 1	Pink
	The Journey		**D**: Dad Mum: **T**: everyone I'm said the	Towards 1	Pink
	Goal!		**D**: Dad got it Mum: **T**: day everyone was a	Towards 1	Red
	Shopping		**D**: got; **T**: ball he she shop shopping some the to wanted a went	Towards 1	Red
	What a Mess!		**D**: Dad Mum; **T**: everyone made some a	Towards 1	Red
	Who Did That?		**D**: Dad did it Mum; **T**: me that she said was wasn't who	Towards 1	Red
St 1+ First Sentences	Hide and Seek		**D**: can dad us yes; **T**: all I me see we you	Towards 1	Pink
	Kipper's Diary		**D**: fun it; **T**: day I park shops the to was went a	Towards 1	Pink
	Look at Me		**D**: at Mum on; **T**: me my no oh look	Towards 1	Pink
	Big Feet		**D**: at big Dad it; **T**: a come no this look is and	Towards 1	Red
	Go Away, Floppy		**T**: are away come go we back	Towards 1	Red
	Reds and Blues		**D**: in on; **T**: is all are come the we who	Towards 1	Red
St 1+ More First Sentences A	What Dogs Like		**D**: run: **T**: like/s play they this to what dogs	Towards 1	Red
	Presents for Dad		**D**: box Dad is it; **T**: a of all best for the this you	Towards 1	Red
	Top Dog		**D**: at big dog top; **T**: look of is a all best like little the this we	Towards 1	Red
	Look After Me		**D**: on up; **T**: after I like me said she the this we went is look	Towards 1	Red
	Go On, Mum!		**D**: am Dad Mum not on; **T**: again go going I said she	Towards 1	Red
	Go Away, Cat		**D**: big cat dog; **T**: a away coming go little no oh is	Towards 1	Red
St1+ More first Sentences B	The Sandcastle		**D**: box in it on had pat top: **T**: a good he said she the was put best	Towards 1	Red
	Floppy's Bone		**D**: big Dad dog Mum ran; **T**: after back a come he no oh said she stop stopped the	Towards 1	Red
	The Box of Treasure		**D**: box Dad had in it; **T**: of a is found he here no said she the was	Towards 1	Red
	Hook a Duck		**D**: big cat dog got had it Mum on; **T**: a go duck he said was what	Towards 1	Red
	Chip's Robot		**D**: box can had it yet; **T**: is a head my no now said see the this we you	Towards 1	Red
	One Wheel		**D**: am at Dad Mum on; **T**: is he I look me no oh one said two three four	Towards 1	Red

Group name/children's initials ....

Biff, Chip and Kipper stories continued

	Title	Date read	Main high frequency words (D = Decodable , T = Tricky)	NC level	Bookband level
St 1 First Phonics	The Ice Cream		**D**: an at big can get on run yes: **T**: come I no oh one look out that the to want	Towards 1	Red
	What a Din!		**D**: big can got has; **T**: a what and	Towards 1	Red
	Can You See Me?		**D**: big can dog if in; **T**: a are look/ing me my of see the tree you	Towards 1	Red
	See Me Skip		**D**: at can Dad on yes; **T**: is look see come day do every go I like me no oh out the this to too way you	Towards 1	Red
	The Mud Pie		**D**: in it not; **T**: a hand my out pie this too water is put	Towards 1	Red
	Good Dog		**D**: am at but can cat dog get if it not sit; **T**: I I'm ball call good me say look see that that's the very you as	Towards 1	Yellow

Songbirds

	Title	Date read	Letters and Sounds phases and example phonic words	NC level	Bookbands level
St 1 Songbirds	Dig, Dig, Dig		Phase 2: dig Tim fun dug lid tin	Towards 1	Pink
	Mum Bug's Bag		Phase 2: Mum bug red bag zip fan	Towards 1	Pink
	Bob Bug		Phase 2: Bob bug big dad fit cup	Towards 1	Pink
	Zack and the Vet		Phase 2: sit Zak did not ran fog	Towards 1	Pink
	Sam's Pot		Phase 2 : Tom got pot Pam Sam pat	Towards 1	Pink
	Top Cat		Phase 2: am top cat pop	Towards 1	Pink

Floppy's Phonics

	Title	Date read	Letters and Sounds phases and example phonic words	NC level	Bookbands level
St 1 Floppy's Phonics	I Can		Phase 2: am mop pop hop top Sam	Towards 1	Pink
	The Dog Tag		Phase 2: cat cap top mop pot tag	Towards 1	Pink
	The Red Hen		Phase 2: tub tin in cat hat tap	Towards 1	Pink
	It!		Phase 2: box rug cap ran bam bad	Towards 1	Pink
	Cat in a Bag		Phase 2: Viv hen not pen bag net	Towards 1	Pink
	Tip Top		Phase 2: box wok pan jug tin mug	Towards 1	Pink

Group name/children's initials ....

Fireflies

	Title	Date read	Main high frequency words (D = Decodable, T = Tricky)	NC level	Bookband level
St1+ Fireflies	This is me		**T**: this is my	Towards 1	Pink
	Dogs		**D**: dog at; **T**: this is look	Towards 1	Pink
	Maya's Family		**D**: am; **T**: this is her I	Towards 1	Pink
	Making Muffins		**D**: In put (north); **T**: I put (south) the	Towards 1	Pink
	Wheels		**T**: here is wheel there are here	Towards 1	Red
	Big and Little		**D**: at it big **T**: look this is little	Towards 1	Red
St1+ More Fireflies	Hop, skip and Jump		**D**: can; **T**: I like to you we	Towards 1	Pink
	Put on a Clown Face		**D**: on put (north); **T**: put (south) the face paint	Towards 1	Pink
	On the Beach		**D**: can on; **T**: I see the a	Towards 1	Pink
	Animal Faces		**D**: it big; **T**: has a	Towards 1	Pink
	The Fire Engine		**T**: this is the fire	Towards 1	Pink
	Clothes for Rain		**D**: at big hat; **T**: look my coat boots	Towards 1	Pink

Snapdragons

	Title	Date read	Main high frequency words (D = Decodable , T = Tricky)	NC level	Bookband level
St1 Snapdragons	My Dad		**D**: Dad on big up got; **T**: put trousers hurry boots jacket gloves fire engine a	Towards 1	Pink
	Going Up and Down		**D**: at up in; **T**: look me I down am going out round dizzy and	Towards 1	Pink
	Where is Baby?		**D**: can jam on but cat mat; **T**: the where baby floor door coat boat bears stairs asleep is I see	Towards 1	Pink
	Breakfast		**T**: you me for the said went cows sheep goats horse hens like eggs I to see	Towards 1	Pink
	My Dog Needs a Bone		**D**: dog big red bed but; **T**: this my like needs bone dish collar lead long a	Towards 1	Pink
	Hello Grandma!		**D**: got in bus on had; **T**: a and we went the to too taxi train plane dinner tea sleep Hello Grandma	Towards 1	Pink

Stages 1 and 1+ checklist of reading skills

Numbers in brackets refer to the Primary National Strategy Literacy *Framework objectives*, e.g. (8.1) means Strand 8, bullet point 1. Points in italics are phase descriptors from the *DCSF Standards Site Phonics Tracker*.

Group .... **Name** ....

Year R Reading skills	Autumn term	Spring term	Summer term
Listen with enjoyment, sustain attentive listening and responds with relevant comments, questions or actions (8.1)			
Show an understanding of the elements of stories, such as main character, sequence of events and openings.(8.2 7.3)			
Know that print carries meaning, and in English, is read from left to right and top to bottom (7.1)			
Retell narratives in the correct sequence, drawing on the language patterns of stories (7.4)			
Link sounds to letters, naming and sounding the letters of the alphabet (5.2)			
Hear and say sounds in words in the order in which they occur (5.5)			
Recognise common digraphs (5.8)			
Read some high frequency words (5.9)			
Recognise and name characters from a story			
explore and experiment with sounds and words			
distinguish between different sounds in the environment and phonemes			
show awareness of rhyme and alliteration			
In addition, at Stage 1+:			
Read a range of familiar and common words and simple sentences independently (5.11)			
Read texts compatible with their phonic knowledge and skills (5.12)			
Read simple words by sounding out and blending the phonemes all through the word from left to right (5.6)			
Recognise when a sentence makes sense			
Recognise words that rhyme			
know that words are constructed from phonemes and that phonemes are represented by graphemes			
know a small selection of common consonants and vowels which they can blend for reading and segment for spelling simple CVC words, for example 'sit' and 'tap'			

Stages 1 and 1+ resources

To teach reading

- Stage 1+ *Songbirds* and *eSongbirds*
- Oxford Reading Tree *Big Talkabout Cards*
- Oxford Reading Tree Stages 1 and 1+ Stories:
  - Stage 1 *Kipper Stories*
  - Stage 1 *Biff and Chip Stories*
  - Stage 1 *First Words*
  - Stage 1 *More First Words*
  - Stage 1+ *First Sentences*
  - Stage 1+ *More First Sentences A*
  - Stage 1+ *More First Sentences B*
  - Stage 1+ *Patterned Stories*
  - Stage 1+ *More Patterned Stories*
  - Stage 1+ *First Phonics*
- Oxford Reading Tree *MagicPage CD-ROM Stages 1-2*
- Stage 1+ *First Sentences Big Books*
- Stages 1-2 *Comprehension Photocopy Masters*
- Stages 1 and 1+ *Story CDs*
- *Sequencing Cards*

For extra practice and consolidation

- Stage 1+ Floppy's Phonics
- Stage 1 and 1+ *Talking Stories*
- Stage 1+ *First Phonics Talking Stories*
- Stage 1+ *Clicker*
- Stages 1-3 *Group Actvity Sheets*
- Stages 1-9 *Phonics and Spelling Actvities*
- *Workbooks 1, 1A* and *1B*
- *Games* Box 1
- *Finger Puppets and Floppy puppet*
- *Oxford Reading Tree Online*

Further reading

- Stage 1+ *Snapdragons*
- Stage 1+ *Fireflies* and *More Fireflies*
- Stage 1+ to 2 *Glow-worms*
- *Rhyme and Analogy First Story Rhymes*

Stage 2 book recording chart

You can use this chart to record books as children read them. It also shows the key information on each book at a glance.

Group name/children's initials ....

Biff, Chip and Kipper stories

	Title	Date read	Main high frequency words (D = Decodable , T = Tricky)	NC level	Bookband level
St 2 Patterned Stories	Creepy-crawly!		**D**: get had in it Mum; **T**: called couldn't out I said she the put	Towards 1	Red
	Monkey Tricks		**D**: at big; **T**: a for like look(ed) the they to went were	Towards 1	Red
	Naughty Children		**D**: an bed had off on up; **T**: came good home oh no said the they two was went what	Towards 1	Red
	Hey Presto!		**D**: big Dad in it Mum on; **T**: called a and her put said she the them to was went	Towards 1	Red
	A Sinking Feeling		**D**: get in on; **T**: couldn't no oh said the were	Towards 1	Red
	It's the Weather		**T**: a day good it's Mrs oh said the was were what	Towards 1	Red
St 2 More Patterned Stories A	The Little Dragon		**D**: am but in will on; **T**: a put went good I like little play said the to what	Towards 1	Red
	The Lost Puppy		**D**: with Dad dog had his it Mum off; **T**: and a called for could couldn't look(ed) Mrs said the they was what	Towards 1	Red
	New Trees		**D**: Dad in it; **T**: give he said she the gave wanted to put was went	Towards 1	Red
	The Band		**D**: at bad Dad dog in; **T**: a couldn't house he his said play(ed) the to went what	Towards 1	Red
	Up and Down		**D**: Dad Mum up; **T**: a and came down see stop went couldn't he said she wanted	Towards 1	Red
	What Is It?		**D**: at it Mum; **T**: he look(ed) said she is was what a and	Towards 1	Red
St 2 Stories	What a Bad Dog!		**D**: Dad dog in Mum on: **T**: what a and down good said went was	Within 1	Yellow
	The Dream		**D**: Dad had it Mum; **T**: couldn't very was her a went	Within 1	Blue
	The Go-kart		**D**: Dad had it Mum; **T**: made go put said the away no stop they wanted a	Within 1	Yellow
	A New Dog		**D**: at big dog too it; **T**: like(d) little look(ed) home the they this wanted was went a	Towards 1	Red
	The Toys' Party		**D**: got Mum; **T**: come he his put wanted was	Towards 1	Red
	New Trainers		**D**: Dad got; **T**: he new no the this to was went wanted	Within 1	Yellow
St 2 More Stories A	The Baby-sitter		**D**: Dad got in; **T**: a back and couldn't go good he his made no said the they to wanted was we went what yes	Within 1	Yellow
	Floppy's Bath		**D**: Dad dog in it Mum got him; **T**: a and looked no put said saw the they took went what	Within 1	Yellow
	Kipper's Balloon		**D**: Dad it Mum on got; **T**: a and he new no said saw to was went	Within 1	Yellow
	Kipper's Birthday		**D**: Dad it Mum on up but with; **T**: stop came a come good made no put said the took wanted was what	Within 1	Yellow
	Spots!		**D**: Dad got had in Mum too; **T**: came a and he looked no out put said she the went what	Within 1	Yellow
	The Water Fight		**D**: Dad with in it Mum got had; **T**: go a at he no said they to wanted stop was wet	Within 1	Yellow

Group name/children's initials ....

Biff, Chip and Kipper stories continued

	Title	Date read	Main high frequency words (D = Decodable , T = Tricky)	NC level	Bookband level
St 2 More Stories B	Biff's Aeroplane		**D**: an it Mum on up; **T**: couldn't good for her looked made she the to wanted was went	Within 1	Yellow
	The Chase		**D**: cat dog it Mum bad got man; **T**: a and good he new said saw some they to wanted was went what you	Within 1	Yellow
	Floppy the Hero		**D**: at dog get had in on see; **T**: a and by back good he little looked out said she some the there to was went what	Within 1	Blue
	Kipper's Laces		**D**: at Dad did had him up; **T**: couldn't a and he his made new no oh said wanted	Within 1	Blue
	The Wobbly Tooth		**D**: Dad hit had it not Mum on; **T**: a and I'm no oh out pull the to said wanted was went	Within 1	Blue
	The Foggy Day		**D**: Dad it Mum got had up; **T**: see a couldn't go home into it's no said saw the they this was were wanted	Within 1	Yellow
St 2 First Phonics	The Big Egg		**D**: an at big Dad too had in Mum on; **T**: and a come he looked me put see said the they went you	Towards 1	Red
	A Present for Mum		**D**: an at can Dad had in Mum: **T**: a come and do for he help said she the wanted was we what	Within 1	Yellow
	The Hole in the Sand		**D**: big Dad got had in it: **T**: all came a and can't day gone good he I let's me new no said stop the they was	Within 1	Yellow
	In a Bit		**D**: an at can Dad had in Mum; **T**: a come do for he help said and she the wanted was we what	Towards 1	Red
	Poor Floppy		**D**: at bad can get had him Mum not on sad; **T**: give he home I looked said she some the to took wanted was went	Within 1	Yellow
	Put It Back		**D**: at back bit Dad had in it Mum on; **T**: a and all come he her is it's let's look no of put said she that the what	Within 1	Yellow

Songbirds

	Title	Date read	Letters and Sounds phases and example phonic words	NC level	Bookband level
St 2 Songbirds	The Odd Pet		Phases 2 and 3: Kim cat Jim zog fat ten	Towards 1	Red
	Singing Dad		Phases 2 and 3: sings long song fishing digging tells off	Towards 1	Red
	Fish and Chips		Phases 2 and 3: chip much fish shop shut whizz	Towards 1	Red
	Miss! Miss!		Phases 2 and 3: Bill will tell Hill doll Miss	Towards 1	Red
	Doctor Duck		Phases 2 and 3: ring rang hopping sick Duck quick	Towards 1	Red
	This and That		Phases 2 and 3: chess Chan shop shell Ship Thin	Towards 1	Red

Group name/children's initials ....

Floppy's Phonics

	Title	Date read	Letters and Sounds phases and example phonic words	NC level	Bookband level
St2 Floppy's Phonics	The Fizz-Buzz		Phases 2 and 3: fizz buzz hiss puff off odd	Towards 1	Red
	Shops		Phases 2 and 3: shell ship shed shall sell will	Towards 1	Red
	The Sing Song		Phases 2 and 3: egg Chip much such cool soon	Towards 1	Red
	Less Mess		Phases 2 and 3: less mess fuss fill well Biff	Towards 1	Red
	The Backpack		Phases 2 and 3: sing song singing dong sang along	Towards 1	Red
	Such a Fuss1		Phases 2 and 3: backpack ducks luck Nick pick cash	Towards 1	Red

Fireflies

	Title	Date read	Main high frequency words (D = Decodable, T = Tricky)	NC level	Bookband level
St2+ Fireflies	Is This Too Much?		**D**: too much yes it not big; **T**: is this no	Towards 1	Pink
	Over and under		**D**: can; **T**: I see you are the	Towards 1	Pink
	Transport		**D**: long; **T**: ago some look(ed) like this now	Towards 1	Red
	Shopping for a Party		**D**: get too; **T**: we have to need some	Towards 1	Red
	Our Class		**D**: in has; **T**: is our class he she	Within 1	Yellow
	Hot and Cold		**D**: hot us; **T**: is makes cold food	Within 1	Yellow
St2+ More Fireflies	Sorting		**D**: can; **T**: I sort them by their the we into	Towards 1	Red
	Boots and Shoes		**T**: here are my I wear when play them	Towards 1	Red
	Diggers		**D**: it big can dig; **T**: this is a digger has and small	Towards 1	Red
	What is This?		**D**: can it an; **T**: you see what this is a or these	Towards 1	Red
	Push and Pull		**D**: Dad Mum pull; **T**: push(es) the pulls my sister all	Towards 1	Red
	Making Prints		**T**: I made used a these to make them prints	Towards 1	Red

Snapdragons

	Title	Date read	Main high frequency words (D = Decodable, T = Tricky)	NC level	Bookband level
St2 Snapdragons	What is it?		**D**: it hat too big; **T**: what is said no a dress small seat wide tunnel help	Towards 1	Red
	The Animal Party		**D**: can dog yes too; **T**: the a to animal party you like I good come my duck all talk	Towards 1	Red
	The Best Sandcastle		**D**: got put (north) on; **T**: the to best sandcastle/s we went made mine no more sand bigger some my now and a	Towards 1	Red
	Don't Jump on the Bed, Fred!		**D**: on off it can bed; **T**: don't jump/ing the like said he down best of all stop want I can't you	Towards 1	Red
	Can You Get Our Ball?		**D**: can get up in Mum Dad on; **T**: you our ball we a went to play the tree look/ed can't was	Towards 1	Red
	Tortoise! Tortoise!		**D**: in up can too; **T**: Tortoise of his was woke I come out my today said no don't it's very now	Towards 1	Red

Stage 2 checklist of reading skills

Numbers in brackets refer to the Primary National Strategy Literacy *Framework objectives*, e.g. (8.1) means Strand 8, bullet point 1. Points in italics are phase descriptors from the *DCSF Standards Site Phonics Tracker.*

Group .... **Name** ....

Year R Reading skills	Autumn term	Spring term	Summer term
Listen with enjoyment (2.1, 8.1)			
Sustain attentive listening responding with relevant comments, questions or actions (2.2)			
Link sounds to letters, naming and sounding the letters of the alphabet (5.2)			
Hear and say sounds in words in the order in which they occur (5.5)			
Read simple words by sounding out and blending the phonemes all through the word from left to right (5.6)			
Recognise common digraphs (5.8)			
Read some high frequency words (5.9)			
Read a range of familiar and common words and simple sentences independently (5.11)			
Read texts compatible with their phonic knowledge and skills (5.12)			
Know that print carries meaning, and in English, is read from left to right and top to bottom (7.1)			
Show an understanding of the elements of stories, such as main character, sequence of events and openings.(7.3, 8.2)			
Retell narratives in the correct sequence, drawing on the language patterns of stories (7.4)			
Read the 26 decodable words and the 7 tricky words listed for Phase 2			
Handle books with confidence, knowing where a story begins and ends			
Use cues from the context and syntax to work out new words			
Locate and read single words within a sentence			
Locate and identify single letters within words			
Recognise when a sentence makes sense			
Know one grapheme for each of the 44 phonemes			
Children can read and spell a few CVC words using a limited range of letters and short vowels, for example 'box			
Children can read and spell CVC words using a wider range of letters, short vowels, some consonant diagraphs and double letters, for example 'bell'			

Stage 2 resources

To teach reading

- Stage 2 *Songbirds* and *eSongbirds*
- Oxford Reading Tree Stage 2 stories:
  - Stage 2 *Stories*
  - Stage 2 *More Stories Pack A*
  - Stage 2 *More Stories Pack B*
  - Stage 2 *Patterned Stories*
  - Stage 2 *Patterned Stories A*
  - Stage 2 *First Phonics*
- Oxford Reading Tree *MagicPage CD-ROM Stages 1-2*
- Stage 2 *Stories Big Books*
- Stages 1-2 *Comprehension Photocopy Masters*
- Stage 2 *Story CDs*
- *Sequencing Cards*
- *Extended Stories*
- *Context Cards*

For extra practice and consolidation

- Stage 2 Floppy's Phonics
- Stage 2 *Talking Stories*
- Stage 2 *First Phonics Talking Stories*
- Stage 2 *Clicker*
- Stages 1-3 *Group Actvity Sheets*
- Stages 1-9 *Phonics and Spelling Actvities*
- *Workbooks 2A, 2B* and *2C*
- *Games* Box 1
- *Finger Puppets and Floppy puppet*
- *Oxford Reading Tree Online*

Further reading

- Stage 2 *Snapdragons*
- Stage 2 *Fireflies* and *More Fireflies*
- Stage 1+ to 2 *Glow-worms*
- *Rhyme and Analogy First Story Rhymes*

Stage 3 book recording chart

You can use this chart to record books as children read them. It also shows the key information on each book at a glance.

Group name/children's initials ....

Biff, Chip and Kipper stories

	Title	Date read	Main high frequency words (D = Decodable , T = Tricky)	NC level	Bookband level
St 3 Stories	On the Sand		**D**: an and looked at cross Dad get on top went; **T**: a hiding made put no played said sleep the they to was	Within 1	Yellow
	The Rope Swing		**D**: at children looked dog went on too; **T**: climbed home no pushed said the they to what	Within 1	Yellow
	By the Stream		**D**: am and children dad fell get in mum on sat see up dropped went; **T**: climbed a couldn't he I played said the they want	Within 1	Yellow
	Nobody Wanted to Play		**D**: am cross his on up went; **T**: climbed a he horse I park play said the to wall wanted was	Within 1	Yellow
	The Egg Hunt		**D**: and at can look for in it mum on tree; **T**: a are hide I like them park said she some the they to where	Within 1	Yellow
	A Cat in the Tree		**D**: at cat cross dad get in on put ran tree up with stuck; **T**: a climbed couldn't everyone he no said she the wall down was	Within 1	Blue
St 3 More Stories A	At the Seaside		**D**: bus but can dad fill had thank help looked his man mum old too went good; **T**: every everyone down family here home said sorry stopped new stay they you he was what	Within 1	Yellow
	Strawberry Jam		**D**: can dad had help his mum pick ran too took; **T**: forgot own put about all everyone car he home make oh over picked said small some they time wanted was were your you	Within 1	Yellow
	The Jumble Sale		**D**: children dad lot mum sad went with; **T**: old out put buy saw toys counted home looked money oh played said something car their they things threw time was wanted was were what	Within 1	Yellow
	The Snowman		**D**: dad children fell good had he mum six took; **T**: children play saw she everyone giant hooray made opened pushed said snowing wanted was	Within 1	Yellow
	Kipper the Clown		**D**: children did fed good had his look man mum drink; **T**: after all be everyone put oh he laugh made me pulled said strong wanted was what	Within 1	Yellow
	Kipper's Idea		**D**: looked children green cross dad for good had into mess may past ran took went; **T**: everyone faces play wall liked painted painting playground school there they wanted was	Within 1	Blue

Group name/children's initials ....

Biff, Chip and Kipper stories *continued*

	Title	Date read	Main high frequency words (D = Decodable , T = Tricky)	NC level	Bookband level
St 3 More Stories B	At the Pool		**D**: and back him his man mum shop too took went; **T**: bought put them they dear for find couldn't everyone home looked new said she sorry wanted was water	Within 1	Yellow
	Book Week		**D**: big book children had week; **T**: ate came dressed put everyone hungry laugh made party picture said there wall was they	Within 1	Yellow
	Bull's-eye!		**D**: book cross dad for got had her hit win went; **T**: ball forgot into they bought couldn't everyone fight kicked said school wanted was watch you won	Within 1	Yellow
	The Barbecue		**D**: children dad food got mum rain went took wet again; **T**: began put cooked everyone fire helped hooray hungry made out outside party said some wanted were	Within 1	Blue
	The Carnival		**D**: children dads good had job mums too took; **T**: car come down everyone put old giant lived looked made many pushed said she there they was were	Within 1	Blue
	The Cold Day		**D**: children wanted dad help mum not ran sat too; **T**: day cold come everyone sea that laugh I'm made played said they was were very looked	Within 1	Blue
St 3 More Stories C	The Ice Rink		**D**: and at Dad Dad's drinks fun got hand held his is jump let look my on sat this went ; **T**: a began cold down go he hold me no oh out put round said some the their they to	Within 1	Yellow
	Pond Dipping		**D**: and at big dad got it let's mum net of on splash stuck up; **T**: a couldn't full made a me old out helped jumped pulled said she some the they was were	Within 1	Yellow
	Sniff		**D**: am and at back cat Dad dog drink duck hot in lost mud mum must on asleep pond ran run stick then up went will fast (N) too took; **T**: a after jumped looked are happy park ball be couldn't fast (S) find for her I liked out roll said she the they to today wanted was were you	Within 1	Yellow
	The Mud Bath		**D**: at bad dad fell in it kick bath (N) mess mud mum on ran splash that up went with; **T**: bath (S) a ball came bathroom called down forgot go he I no oh over said the there to TV was want what playing looked	Within 1	Yellow
	The Steel Band		**D**: and as band bang can clap feet hands help hit in it man sang sing song tap up us with children; **T**: name my play a all don't everyone he I now put said to their wants wanted what came who you your is	Within 1	Yellow
	The Duck Race		**D**: an dad's drop ducks get got had in it let's mum off on six stick stuck went past (N) fast (N) with; **T**: a began down fast (S) have landed made no oh past (S) race said the they two	Within 1	Blue

Group name/children's initials ....

Songbirds

	Title	Date read	Letters and Sounds phases and example phonic words	NC level	Bookband level
St 3 Songbirds	Gran is Cross		Phases 3 and 4: twins gran Flick brings pram Fred	Within 1	Yellow
	The Scrap Rocket		Phases 3 and 4: plug pump plank spring strap string	Within 1	Yellow
	The Trunk and the Skunk		Phases 3 and 4: stamp tramp crash trunk lift drink	Within 1	Yellow
	The Shopping List		Phases 3 and 4: went bank next lift pink golf	Within 1	Yellow
	Splash and Squelch		Phases 3 and 4: swing spin splish splosh sand squirrels	Within 1	Yellow
	The Big Match		Phases 3 and 4: sing rings duck quack kick Rick	Within 1	Yellow
St 3 More Songbirds	Ron Rabbit's Big Day		Phases 3 and 4: needs three sees green asleep creeping	Within 1	Yellow
	Bob Bug and the Insect Club		Phases 3 and 4: toast toad toads cockroach roast	Within 1	Yellow
	The Wishing Elf		Phases 3 and 4: flies pie tries tie	Within 1	Yellow
	Where is the Snail?		Phases 3 and 4: snail sails tail wait	Within 1	Yellow
	Stop Chatting, Bill		Phases 3 and 4: too smooth tooth	Within 1	Yellow
	Back to Bed		Phases 3 and 4: look wooden book books foot good	Within 1	Yellow

Floppy's Phonics

	Title	Date read	Letters and Sounds phases and example phonic words	NC level	Bookband level
St 3 Floppy's Phonics	The Moon Jet		Phases 3 and 4: moon cool zoom boom room roof	Within 1	Yellow
	Quick, Quick		Phases 3 and 4: quick jack the this ball will	Within 1	Yellow
	Wet Feet		Phases 3 and 4: feet deep feed need reel feel	Within 1	Yellow
	The Red Coat		Phases 3 and 4: coat soap foam soak load king	Within 1	Yellow
	Rain Again		Phases 3 and 4: rain again pain pail nail wait	Within 1	Yellow
	The Rook and the Ring		Phases 3 and 4: look rook good took cooking wood	Within 1	Yellow

Group name/children's initials ....

Fireflies

	Title	Date read	Main high frequency words (D = Decodable, T = Tricky)	NC level	Bookband level
St 3 Fireflies	Football, Football		**D**: on in at; **T**: I play football the with our my	Within 1	Yellow
	Choices		**D**: paint; **T**: likes to play the he she read quietly make write grow	Within 1	Yellow
	Going Somewhere		**D**: did on; **T**: we are going could we what to a take else	Towards 1	Red
	How to Draw Yourself		**D**: can look at on; **T**: you draw a picture yourself a the your line(s) hair	Within 1	Yellow
	How to Be Healthy		**D**: too lots am; **T** :day healthy I that me eat of every	Within 1	Yellow
	My Week		**D**: went lunch with lots of; **T**: I to school story my a was read the	Within 1	Yellow
St 3 More Fireflies	Jumpers		**D**: jump of on help strong leg back them tail; **T**: are the they out to for their have jumper water	Within 1	Yellow
	Making a Road		**D**: this track truck flat and it big road; **T**: machine/s for make/s a the rolls over here makes stones	Within 1	Yellow
	Floating Boats		**D**: Put (N) in this will sink/s it them float; **T**: The some a what no water clay we boats bowl put (S)	Within 1	Yellow
	Patterns		**D**: this is wing/s lock on sand; **T**: a like pattern/s for butterfly made the ground leaves snowflake some	Within 1	Yellow
	Mirrors		**D**: Can see in this look big is too at; **T**: I mirror a like funny upside down my we me	Within 1	Yellow
	The School Band		**D**: look up and in drum; **T**: I play we how down move fingers my out	Within 1	Yellow

Snapdragons

	Title	Date read	Main high frequency words (D = Decodable, T = Tricky)	NC level	Bookband level
St 3 Snapdragons	Grandma's Glasses		**D**: and in his too on then but lost help; **T**: came Grandma's looked to her Grandpa the she saw glasses	Within 1	Yellow
	The Singing Bird		**D**: in this too went up; **T**: the a for singing bird there was little she happy everyone saw said some very	Within 1	Yellow
	New Blue Shoes		**D**: on too will get went but put (N); **T**: her into a new blue shoes put (S) they were are said we you some	Within 1	Yellow
	Presents for Baby		**D**: Mum went to took had Dad see and him with Grandad hospital; **T**: a for presents baby Grandma came stay boy the that's	Within 1	Yellow
	Melting Snow		**D**: got and melting it's let's; **T**: a to snow snowing make snowman everyone came out want the said bigger smaller was	Within 1	Yellow
	A House for Hedgehog		**D**: is too went look need but (N) it on; **T**: a house for he to my hedgehog I so new said	Within 1	Yellow

Stage 4 book recording chart

You can use this chart to record books as children read them. It also shows the key information on each book at a glance.

Group name/children's initials ....

Biff, Chip and Kipper stories

	Title	Date read	Main high frequency words (D = Decodable , T = Tricky)	NC level	Bookband level
St 4 Stories	House for Sale		**D**: a and at bed big can down for in it mum on room sat this too tree up went pulled; **T**: chair chimney into climbed down looked jumped everyone garden house liked the they wanted was	Within 1	Blue
St 4 Stories	The New House		**D**: a and at big box came children dad he his in job lot man mum no of oh play soon things too van went put (N); **T**: come helped looked everyone goodbye house new put (S) said to the they toys what	Within 1	Blue
St 4 Stories	Come In!		**D**: a came children Dad five cross for gave home in looked lot of mum play she three mess painting to went with; **T**: biscuits come four house out outside said some television they wanted was watching were what	Within 1	Blue
St 4 Stories	The Secret Room		**D**: a and at bed dad dog her him in it job like looks mum off on asleep room she shop stuck things three too us inside went fast (N); **T**: about door dreamed everyone fast (S) found house little new opened our pulled said looked liked the they this was what wanted into to	Within 1	Blue
St 4 Stories	The Play		**D**: a and away came dads dog fun gave go he her him home in it it's like man class (N) met mums of on time too went inside put (N); **T**: helped about class (S) played couldn't flowers girl house liked little outside painted playtime put (S) said school some storm story there to they was were what	Within 1	Blue
St 4 Stories	The Storm		**D**: a and at bed box came dad dads for go had he her his home in it mum mums mess no oh on room things time to inside tree went wind; **T**: blew down climbed door everyone found good house key opened outside helped said school something storm there they wanted was what looked mended	Within 1	Green
St 4 More Stories A	The Balloon		**D**: an by wrong came children everyone gave good home made outside prize time took idea; **T**: Mrs liked school were what down houses park saw shouted wanted watch	Within 1	Green
St 4 More Stories A	The Camcorder		**D**: came children day got had her made make men race running smile them took tree phone; **T**: easy everyone laughed showed two were shouted call house saw wanted	Within 1	Green
St 4 More Stories A	Nobody Got Wet		**D**: but good got had help home out rain time wet; **T**: don't everyone nobody what pulled pushed down	Within 1	Blue
St 4 More Stories A	Poor Old Mum!		**D**: came day good had jump last long old put second shouted; **T**: everyone first hooray poor third	Within 1	Yellow
St 4 More Stories A	The Wedding		**D**: been came happy his joke made not put (N) them took be will; **T**: don't everyone there want helped liked put (S)	Within 1	Blue
St 4 More Stories A	The Weather Vane		**D**: an back but came had man roof take took idea; **T**: be jumped what over	Within 1	Blue

Group name/children's initials ....

Biff, Chip and Kipper stories *continued*

	Title	Date read	Main high frequency words (D = Decodable , T = Tricky)	NC level	Bookband level
St 4 More Stories B	The Dragon Dance		**D**: an big came children did good got had her inside long made them upset be don't idea **T**: everyone head half people school tore wanted what helped dance liked	Within 1	Blue
	The Flying Elephant		**D**: an back children fat flat sorry man strong that took away don't; **T**: laughed school want liked now	Within 1	Yellow
	Everyone Got Wet		**D**: again came children fell got help off old put (N) tap top very wet; **T**: new water wanted what down out over put (S)	Within 1	Yellow
	Wet Paint		**D**: again an back children had hands his inside old put (N) open; **T**: there wanted were what ball put (S) jumped pushed door here outside	Within 1	Yellow
	The Scarf		**D**: came children good had help her long made make not off put (N) sorry ran safe stop took idea; **T**: put (S) couldn't everyone some threw what boy liked pulled out shouted	Within 1	Blue
	Swap!		**D**: black bike good had his not put (N); T: new wheels helped put (S) found liked now	Within 1	Yellow

Group name/children's initials ....

Songbirds

	Title	Date read	Letters and Sounds phases and example phonic words	NC level	Bookband level
St 4 Songbirds	Moan, Moan Moan!		Phase 5: moans coat soap coal toast road	Within 1	Blue
St 4 Songbirds	Queen Anneena's Feast		Phase 5: queen fifteen green seen see sweet	Within 1	Blue
St 4 Songbirds	The Snake and the Drake		Phase 5: rainy tail raisins wait day away	Within 1	Blue
St 4 Songbirds	Tadpoles		Phase 5: see weeds eats jelly baby tiny	Within 1	Blue
St 4 Songbirds	Spike Says		Phase 5: fight night spy fly sky pie	Within 1	Blue
St 4 Songbirds	The Wrong Kind of Knight		Phase 5: need knees freezing Kareem read hurry	Within 1	Blue
St 4 More Songbirds	The Red Man and the Green Man		Phase 5: again snail train day holiday say	Within 1	Blue
St 4 More Songbirds	Pirates		Phase 5: sail wait away play Jade Wakes	Within 1	Blue
St 4 More Songbirds	Tails		Phase 5: whale bobtail tail away stingray shapes	Within 1	Blue
St 4 More Songbirds	Pen-Pals		Phase 5: afraid friday may game name reading	Within 1	Blue
St 4 More Songbirds	My Cat		Phase 5: keeps feeling sea me silly suddenly	Within 1	Blue
St 4 More Songbirds	Tim's Bad Mood		Phase 5: mood bedroom food spoon too stool	Within 1	Blue

Floppy's Phonics

	Title	Date read	Letters and Sounds phases and example phonic words	NC level	Bookband level
St 4 Floppy's Phonics	Seasick		Phase 5: beach near sea seats each cream	Within 1	Blue
St 4 Floppy's Phonics	Egg Fried Rice		Phase 5: fried rice tried cried quite right	Within 1	Blue
St 4 Floppy's Phonics	The Knight Who Was Afraid		Phase 5: knight knit knees knocked not name	Within 1	Blue
St 4 Floppy's Phonics	Craig Saves the Day		Phase 5: Craig Gail wait tails day Haygate	Within 1	Blue
St 4 Floppy's Phonics	Joe		Phase 5: Joe coal toe oats loaf roast	Within 1	Blue
St 4 Floppy's Phonics	Dolphin Rescue		Phase 5: dolphin phone photo fin why lying	Within 1	Blue

Group name/children's initials ....

Fireflies

	Title	Date read	Main high frequency words (D = Decodable, T = Tricky)	NC level	Bookband level
St 4 Fireflies	Shells		**D**: shell snail keep safe helps crab clam is this with inside; **T**: outside turtle live(s) the move part	Within 1	Blue
	Night Animals		**D**: animals night food sleep day eat at awake; **T**: nocturnal are they their	Within 1	Green
	Grandad and Me		**D**: my grandad I am is playing a good made class cream (N); **T**: toy house here school class (S) ice car favourite photo outside	Within 1	Green
	World Instruments		**D**: man is blow hard drums to very has in made he she music this; **T**: people live(s) the	Towards 2	Orange
	From Curry to Rice		**D**: can be green foods start with find; **T**: different are they sour small dictionary other taste yellow letter(s) often you	Towards 2	Orange
	Shapes		**D**: flat same a can see side; **T**: some you how have triangle pyramid square rectangle angles faces edges are the many	Towards 2	Turquoise
St 4 More Fireflies	Big cats		**D**: big cats lion(s) run fast hunt very good can see in at; **T**: are leopards live their world tigers forest(s)	Within 1	Blue
	Animal Feet		**D**: feet on help them sticky toes; **T**: have their fur to	Within 1	Blue
	How to Make a Fruit Salad		**D**: good put (N) in and shopping make it salad basket; **T**: fruit some the juice your you into put (N)	Within 1	Blue
	How to Make a Puppet Theatre		**D**: play box it in cut on paint card; **T**: the some draw colour glue bridge	Within 1	Blue
	Hello		**D**: hello I my me send(s) back say Mum wave an a he email write; **T**: message to writes brother goodbye	Within 1	Blue
	Ballet		**D**: go up I foot then my; **T**: ballet class we love the down music point	Within 1	Blue

Snapdragons

	Title	Date read	Main high frequency words (D = Decodable, T = Tricky)	NC level	Bookband level
St 4 Snapdragons	An Old Red Hat		**D**: an old red hat had got in go off this nest eggs; **T**: have there said saw you	Within 1	Blue
	Mr Fox's Socks		**D**: made took home put (N) them socks night; **T**: saw looked some they warm about come mice put (S)	Within 1	Blue
	No Problem!		**D**: like take back went help don't; **T**: what looked bought jacket there were friend people about said	Within 1	Blue
	The Mouse with No Name		**D**: with came this into off children name; **T**: mouse school one little chased there said could down looked	Within 1	Blue
	Little Mouse Deer and the Crocodile		**D**: went help make made crocodile; **T**: little mouse deer could other there was wanted want many said river jumped	Within 1	Blue
	The Tortoise and the Baboon		**D**: took long last must across baboon back; **T**: tortoise wanted come house walked was laughed dinner first	Within 1	Blue

Stage 4 checklist of reading skills

Numbers in brackets refer to the Primary National Strategy *Literacy Framework* objectives, e.g. (8.2) means Strand 8, bullet point 2. Points in italics are phase descriptors from the *DCSF Standards Site Phonics Tracker.*

Group .... **Name** ....

Year 1 Reading skills	Autumn term	Spring term	Summer term
Identify the constituent parts of two-syllable and three-syllable words to support the application of phonic knowledge and skills (5.3)			
Recognise automatically an increasing number of familiar high-frequency words (5.4)			
Apply phonic knowledge and skills as the prime approach to reading and spelling unfamiliar words that are not completely decodable (5.5)			
Read more challenging texts which can be decoded using their acquired phonic knowledge and skills, along with automatic recognition of high frequency words (5.6)			
Read and spell phonetically decodable two-syllable and three-syllable words (5.7, 6.6)			
Identify the main events and characters in stories, and find specific information in simple texts (7.1)			
Use syntax and context when reading for meaning (7.2)			
Make predictions showing an understanding of ideas, events and characters (7.3)			
Recognise the main elements that shape different texts (7.4)			
Visualise and comment on events, characters and ideas, making imaginative links to their own experiences (8.2)			
Enjoy reading stories, using both the pictures and the text to fully understand the story			
Talk about why things happen in the stories			
Make inferences about characters' feelings and motives			
Begin to read with expression			
Children can use alternative ways of pronouncing and spelling the graphemes corresponding to the long vowel phonemes, for example /oe/ o-e, o, oa, ow, e.g. 'snake'			
Children can read phonically decodable two-syllable and three-syllable words, for example 'bleating', 'frogspawn', 'shopkeeper'			

Stage 4 resources

To teach reading

- Stage 4 *Songbirds*, Stage 4 *More Songbirds* and *eSongbirds*
- Oxford Reading Tree Stage 4 stories:
  - Stage 4 *Stories*
  - Stage 4 *More Stories Pack A*
  - Stage 4 *More Stories Pack B*
  - Stage 4 *More Stories Pack C*
- Oxford Reading Tree *MagicPage CD-ROM Stages 3–5*
- Stages 3–5 *Comprehension Photocopy Masters*
- Stage 4 *Story CDs*
- *Sequencing Cards*
- *Extended Stories*
- *Context Cards*

For extra practice and consolidation

- Stage 4 *Floppy's Phonics*
- Stage 4 *Sparrows*
- Stage 4 *Talking Stories*
- Stage 4 *Clicker*
- Stages 4–5 *Group Activity Sheets*
- Stages 1–9 *Phonics and Spelling Activities*
- Stage 4 *Workbooks 4A* and *4B*
- *Games* Box 2
- *Finger Puppets* and *Floppy puppet*
- *Oxford Reading Tree Online*

Further reading

- Stage 4 *Snapdragons*
- Stage 4 *Fireflies* and *More Fireflies*
- Stages 3–4 *Glow-worms*
- *Rhyme and Analogy Story Rhymes*
- *All Stars* Packs 1, 1A, 2, and 2A
- *Robins* Pack 1
- *Traditional Tales* (age 6–7)

Stage 5 book recording chart

You can use this chart to record books as children read them. It also shows the key information on each book at a glance.

Group name/children's initials ....

Biff, Chip and Kipper stories

	Title	Date read	Main high frequency words (D = Decodable , T = Tricky)	NC level	Bookband level
St 5 Stories	The Magic Key		**D**: by couldn't house; **T**: adventure	Within 1	Blue
	Pirate Adventure		**D**: came don't house I'm put time climbed frightened; **T**: goodbye working	Within 1	Green
	The Dragon Tree		**D:** about came couldn't don't put time didn't frightened; **T**: adventure working	Within 1	Green
	Gran		**D**: about came don't house made old Gran's yelled; **T**: adventure football working	Within 1	Green
	Castle Adventure		**D**: came couldn't don't old put time; **T**: adventures castle goodbye people	Within 1	Green
	Village in the Snow		**D**: about made put boy's fight time lovely; **T**: adventure Mrs school village working saw	Within 1	Green
St 5 More Stories A	The Great Race		**D**: back came help home man new not now found put race that them too took way would will with wanted what glowed little; **T**: called dangerous signpost	Within 1	Green
	A Monster Mistake		**D**: back but came don't from had brilliant just made make man next now put time with holiday painted wanted what; **T**: believe here television there saw were	Within 1	Blue
	It's Not Fair		**D**: boys but can't got had her brilliant here his it's new couldn't idea lived not teacher now over put time about wanted want; **T**: adventure call saw girl	Towards 2	Orange
	Underground Adventure		**D**: but came don't down good has have our out put ran them there time took want way were some what idea secret; **T**: adventure beautiful cellar laughed people call	Within 1	Green
	Vanishing Cream		**D**: back but came don't had help her him his home house made out put ran bottle some them then time took will want wrong bedroom climbed; **T**: school theatre were	Within 1	Green
	The Whatsit		**D**: but came don't found good got had house lady brilliant look man need looked jumped new off museum old put sheet they took what asked (N) wanted; **T**: asked (S) ceiling ghost surprise walls door	Within 1	Green
St 5 More Stories B	Camping Adventure		**D**: back bed boy could cows down farm has had help couldn't house last may milk new ran them tree very will hospital; **T**: adventure car doctor field laughed there what worse here storm they	Within 1	Green
	A New Classroom		**D**: but came for had may put saw then want was wanted what will excited about upside photograph looked right; **T**: knew oh people talked watched they	Within 1	Green
	Mum to the Rescue		**D**: can children dad down get help lady mum out family holiday nobody put she careful climbed wanted time went what; **T**: asked (S) brought dangerous rescue	Within 1	Green
	The New Baby		**D**: about and boy brilliant can had help her how made off old that time told some too will with want what wheel when hospital looked pleased; **T**: brought called puzzled school new	Within 1	Green
	Noah's Ark Adventure		**D**: about boys brilliant but about call girl couldn't got idea teacher had his it's not now over put time want brilliant lived wanted; **T**: adventure can't saw here	Within 1	Green
	Scarecrows		**D**: boy girl had know old put them was she went little wanted couldn't with alive glowed helped looked planted (N); **T**: oh planted (S) there weren't we're they	Within 1	Green

Group name/children's initials ....

Biff, Chip and Kipper stories continued

	Title	Date read	Main high frequency words (D = Decodable , T = Tricky)	NC level	Bookband level
St 5 More Stories C	Sleeping Beauty		**D**: asleep fast (N) free began help everything man picked knows then over thick way what woke; **T**: sharp ate adventure beauty door everywhere these working	Within 1	Green
	The Adventure Park		**D**: across back big down home table next phone rope wanted sky hungry this tree with front; **T**: beautiful busy here there were flew	Within 1	Green
	Kipper and the Trolls		**D**: cut didn't going food hands into last mud out room have likes be looked began what will come; **T**: after (S) fair first oh pie were hooray	Within 1	Green
	Safari Adventure		**D**: away back around began couldn't didn't exciting good hid home men chased idea ran see suddenly them won't this tree went; **T**: after (S) asked (S) called here oh why catch they	Within 1	Green
	Dad's Run		**D**: children fun had help him bikes keep long need good now old running times way well will with come every idea went; **T**: four hooray ouch park poor can't	Within 1	Green
	Drawing Adventure		**D**: began cross get glad helped good magic like must only ran red run sorry they top yelled come gasped (N) over quick rope; **T**: everywhere gasped (S) ones their were drawings	Within 1	Green

Songbirds

	Title	Date read	Letters and Sounds phases and example phonic words	NC level	Bookband level
St 5 Songbirds	Sue Kangaroo		Phase 5: school kangaroo moon balloons spoons toot	Within 1	Green
	The Cinderella Play		Phase 5: see bossy ugly he she tight	Within 1	Green
	Usman's Books		Phase 5: bookshelf books cookery good flood woodcutter	Within 1	Green
	The Upside-Down Browns		Phase 5: brown down shower towel crown powder	Within 1	Green
	Leroy		Phase 5: coins toilet voice noisy spoils boy	Within 1	Green
	No Milk Today		Phase 5: green needed feet freeze sheep feed	Within 1	Green

Group name/children's initials ....

Fireflies

	Title	Date read	Main high frequency words (D = Decodable, T = Tricky)	NC level	Book band level
St 5 Fireflies	Magic Tricks		**D**: magic tricks this finger(s) spoon wand amaze number hand rubber bottle thumb; **T**: friends your you	Towards 2	Orange
	E-Mails Home		**D**: I thanks having trip went long sand e-mail was; **T**: building(s) walk great all where morning built guess palace saw	Towards 2	Orange
	Looking after Your Dog		**D**: after dog need dry food water clean bowl(s) shampoo lead wash play brush; **T**: healthy place hose kennel	Towards 2	Turquoise
	Public Art		**D**: public can be made sound graffiti hotel shapes trees toilet lights ice; **T**: art carvings statue(s) sculpture(s)	Towards 2	Turquoise
	Houses Then and Now		**D**: rooms family old had has is bathroom(s) washing this bedroom new house was; **T**: houses built friends kitchen here	Towards 2	Turquoise
	Wonders of the World		**D**: Very reef look at map rock(s) deep river(s) deepest mountain(s); **T**: where island glacier world desert largest waterfall	Within 2	Gold
St 5 More Fireflies	Sharks		**D**: hunts biggest eat water teeth live they whale hundreds is; **T**: shark(s) near small out fishes are	Within 1	Green
	Unusual Birds		**D**: wings nest(s) egg(s) they beak pelican water feet sleep fly food long eat like flap legs necks; **T**: birds their penguin(s)	Within 1	Green
	How to Make a Wormery		**D**: home put layers what sand leaves grass (N) do top soil will look some; **T**: worms wormery	Within 1	Green
	The Seaside Then and Now		**D**: seaside ago sun then trip children hundred families clothes shows now photos today; **T**: years were people walking one are there	Within 1	Green
	Volcanoes		**D**: rock volcano erupts some very melted plants trees animals into hot it in ash; **T**: lava people are	Within 1	Green
	Julia Donaldson A Biography		**D**: she rabbit children book(s) old lived loved liked song(s) act sister when poems plays; **T**: stories years school orange	Within 1	Green

Snapdragons

	Title	Date read	Main high frequency words (D = Decodable, T = Tricky)	NC level	Book banc level
St 5 Snapdragons	Locked Out		**D**: home again help too come looked key suddenly what house; **T**: walked where door were laughed through	Within 1	Green
	Little Dragon		**D**: could dragon soon went they fast very didn't liked came little; **T**: their can't school laughed learned	Within 1	Green
	Alf Saves the Day		**D**: day good played children loved very every suddenly everything wanted other; **T**: football people were one everyone	Within 1	Green
	The School Trip		**D**: last went wanted animals them back took away help come have noise little; **T**: school there first	Within 1	Green
	The Chatterbox Turtle		**D**: chatterbox animals came lived asked looked they home wanted could back with must what; **T**: saw can't turtle there where	Within 1	Green
	The Sandwich that Jack Made		**D**: made some put then with little found; **T**: here all	Within 1	Green

Stage 5 checklist of reading skills

Numbers in brackets refer to the Primary National Strategy *Literacy Framework* objectives, e.g. (8.2) means Strand 8, bullet point 2. Points in italics are phase descriptors from the *DCSF Standards Site Phonics Tracker.*

Group .... **Name** ....

Year 1 Reading skills	Autumn term	Spring term	Summer term
Recognise and use alternative ways of pronouncing graphemes already taught (e.g. *g* in 'get' and 'gem', *ow* in 'how' and 'show' (5.1)			
Identify the constituent parts of two-syllable and three-syllable words to support the application of phonic knowledge and skills (5.3)			
Recognise automatically an increasing number of familiar high-frequency words (5.4)			
Apply phonic knowledge and skills as the prime approach to reading and spelling unfamiliar words that are not completely decodable (5.5)			
Read more challenging texts which can be decoded using their acquired phonic knowledge and skills, along with automatic recognition of high frequency words (5.6)			
Read and spell phonetically decodable two-syllable and three-syllable words (5.7, 6.6)			
Identify the main events and characters in stories, and find specific information in simple texts (7.1)			
Use syntax and context when reading for meaning (7.2)			
Make predictions showing an understanding of ideas, events and characters (7.3)			
Recognise the main elements that shape different texts (7.4)			
Visualise and comment on events, characters and ideas, making imaginative links to their own experiences (8.2)			
Read with increasing fluency and enjoyment, using appropriate expression			
Talk about why things happen in the stories			
Make inferences about characters' feelings and motives			
Refer to other stories when discussing the events and characters			
Express an opinion about what they like and dislike in stories			
Recognise that commas, exclamation marks and question marks show us how to read the text			
Children can read phonically decodable two-syllable and three-syllable words, for example 'bleating', 'frogspawn', 'shopkeeper'			
Children can spell complex words using phonically plausible attempts			

Stage 5 resources

To teach reading

- Stage 5 *Songbirds* and *eSongbirds*
- Oxford Reading Tree Stage 5 stories:
  - Stage 5 *Stories*
  - Stage 5 *More Stories Pack A*
  - Stage 5 *More Stories Pack B*
  - Stage 5 *More Stories Pack C*
- Oxford Reading Tree *MagicPage CD-ROM Stages 3–5*
- Stages 3–5 *Comprehension Photocopy Masters*
- Stage 5 *Story CDs*
- Context Cards

For extra practice and consolidation

- Stage 5 *Floppy's Phonics*
- Stage 5 *Talking Stories*
- Stage 5 *Clicker*
- Stages 4–5 *Group Activity Sheets*
- Stages 1–9 *Phonics and Spelling Activities*
- Stage 5 *Workbooks 5A* and *5B*
- *Games* Box 2
- *Finger Puppets*
- *Floppy puppet*
- *Oxford Reading Tree Online*

Further reading

- Stage 5 *Snapdragons*
- Stage 5 *Fireflies* and *More Fireflies*
- Stage 5–6 *Glow-worms*
- *Rhyme and Analogy Story Rhymes*
- *All Stars* Packs 1, 1A, 2, and 2A
- *Robins* Pack 1
- *Traditional Tales* (age 6–7)

Stage 6 book recording chart

You can use this chart to record books as children read them. It also shows the key information on each book at a glance.

Group name/children's initials ....

Biff, Chip and Kipper stories

	Title	Date read	Main high frequency words (D = Decodable , T = Tricky)	NC level	Bookband level
St 6 Stories	Land of the Dinosaurs		**D**: came camera found good could didn't climbed flew don't our photograph push down film hide hill house hurt just land long meet must picked silly took water won't some another called museum; **T**: one school fierce eat	Towards 2	Orange
	In the Garden		**D**: came don't down drops climb grass help here house inside must outside over very called giant love mend pulled pushed rain; **T**: can't	Within 1	Green
	Kipper and the Giant		**D**: adventure out angry giant nobody back pointed threw tiny bigger boy came don't called help house lived old over roofs saw stone time took very want; **T**: again castle one people their	Towards 2	Orange
	The Outing		**D**: about back came couldn't didn't don't home called home hope lady museum lions make near picked showed some silly time photograph pictures told water; **T**: school shoe	Towards 2	Turquoise
	Robin Hood		**D**: about again black by came catch could don't down free got had help her here how just lived made must over saw seen so take that them three time too us some suddenly what want will with called do new next nobody; **T**: can't one people there where who	Towards 2	Orange
	The Treasure Chest		**D**: about after been came couldn't didn't don't down had how now old over saw seen ten little lovely many more new next our out pulled pushed some surprise that them time too what took very want with air called close; **T**: dangerous there thought were who	Towards 2	Turquoise
St 6 More Stories A	Rotten Apples		**D**: about by came everything made put saw excited looked noise suddenly wanted asked; **T**: bought gone laughed	Towards 2	Orange
	Christmas Adventure		**D**: came don't here house made put time your asked computer tomorrow wanted; **T**: television	Towards 2	Orange
	The Go-kart Race		**D**: about day don't made make old painted put saw time asked liked suddenly worry	Towards 2	Orange
	A Fright in the Night		**D**: by came don't house glowed light made make idea loved noise night old saw time very before called; **T**: heard	Towards 2	Orange
	The Laughing Princess		**D**: about adventure could don't made make put saw asked idea looked notice groaned; **T**: caught	Towards 2	Orange
	The Shiny Key		**D**: about adventure bright came crossly here made put saw very your careful climbed helped somebody; **T**: beautiful thief thought	Towards 2	Orange
St 6 More Stories B	Dad's Grand Plan		**D**: came couldn't day don't made make put saw time family holiday looked moaned nothing thirsty whispered wrong; **T**: clothes	Towards 2	Orange
	Mirror Island		**D**: could don't here I'm made put saw time your adventure asked called downstairs frightened idea looked opened terrible	Towards 2	Orange
	Don't be Silly		**D**: about came could don't here I'm made put saw time pulled yelled pushed quietly called holiday; **T**: bought someone true	Towards 2	Orange

Group name/children's initials ....

Biff, Chip and Kipper stories *continued*

	Title	Date read	Main high frequency words (D = Decodable, T = Tricky)	NC level	Bookband level
St 6 More Stories C	Paris Adventure		**D**: after came can't down how little make must one over pull some than there time took wanted night with; **T**: people were where	Towards 2	Orange
	Olympic Adventure		**D**: about after boy could crown girl have her here jump man name next not put ran should so time took tree history museum prizes; **T**: guards were who one	Towards 2	Orange
	Ship in Trouble		**D**: can't from girl help house last must name danger next our out over called exciting love first have what playground pull put should so time took us wanted; **T**: people there	Towards 2	Orange
	The Stolen Crown Part 1		**D**: about after been could crown don't door become good how just last makes must old have put saw where time take took very climb; **T**: castle guards once search who	Towards 2	Orange
	The Stolen Crown Part 2		**D**: after been can't could crown don't from how just much must now out glass want what over put were saw take them then these time took have; **T**: guards two one who	Towards 2	Orange
	Homework!		**D**: animal can't cast don't door from her home how next not our out over put when nature little what some time took tree called diary want way; **T**: autumn half were	Towards 2	Orange

Songbirds

	Title	Date read	Letters and Sounds phases and example phonic words	NC level	Bookband level
St 6 Songbirds	Clare and the Fair		Phase 5: fair chair air hair stare Clare	Towards 2	Orange
	Tara's Party		Phase 5: Tara party cards March car scarf	Towards 2	Orange
	Paula the Vet		Phase 5: torn thorn morning ordinary extraordinary Paula	Towards 2	Orange
	The Deer and the Earwig		Phase 5: hear ear earwig dear fear spear	Towards 2	Orange
	Jack and the Giants		Phase 5: tour sure tourists creature he we	Towards 2	Orange
	Where Were You, Bert?		Phase 5: Bert her caterpillar mermaid furry nurse	Towards 2	Orange

Group name/children's initials ....

Fireflies

	Title	Date read	Main high frequency words (D = Decodable, T = Tricky)	NC level	Book band level
St 6 Fireflies	Wild Weather		**D**: wild cloud(s) thunder air flash strong weather flood rain hail storm thunderstorm storm tornado hurricane lightning; **T**: dangerous	Within 2	Purple
	Unusual Buildings		**D**: houses made glass ago long time bricks would bottles space unusual pyramids; **T**: people warm built build buildings builders	Within 2	Purple
	Tour de France		**D**: bike rider team(s) mountains fastest cyclist flat rider fast day hills France each race; **T**: tyre(s) through jersey stage(s)	Within 2	Purple
	Food as Art		**D**: picture sculpture furniture artist stuck made painted food cakes this shows from very different photograph walls; **T**: people	Within 2	Purple
	Skateboarding		**D**: street race trick ramp jump(s) scooters ground middle off on wheels air rollerskates; **T**: skateboarding skateboard(s) board	Within 2	Gold
	Dinosaurs		**D**: big brain(s) carnivores herbivores eggs beak feet teeth fossils bird ate years taller; **T**: dinosaurs Earth	Within 2	Gold

Snapdragons

	Title	Date read	Main high frequency words (D = Decodable, T = Tricky)	NC level	Book band level
St 6 Snapdragons	The House that Jack Built		**D**: house that place here began found with made went inside these more wanted; **T**: build/built where	Towards 2	Orange
	Sam Sorts it Out		**D**: very down called another wish went took found under first good about can't; **T**: were laughed worked	Towards 2	Orange
	Batter Splatter!		**D**: children when wanted coming some head careful good must couldn't called looked; **T**: school laughed through another	Towards 2	Orange
	Something So Big		**D**: lived come didn't help that head here everything something; **T**: friend one somewhere there thought	Towards 2	Orange
	The Samosa Thief		**D**: could very down them some asked samosa really; **T**: thief everyone great thought were laughed gone	Towards 2	Orange
	The Mole who was Scared of the Dark		**D**: dark mole looked something wouldn't really only under about different never help down found very nothing; **T**: were	Towards 2	Orange

Stage 6 checklist of reading skills

Numbers in brackets refer to the Primary National Strategy *Literacy Framework* objectives, e.g. (8.2) means Strand 8, bullet point 2. Points in italics are phase descriptors from the *DCSF Standards Site Phonics Tracker.*

Group .... **Name** ....

Year 2 Reading skills	Autumn term	Spring term	Summer term
Read independently and with increasing fluency longer and less familiar texts (5.1)			
Know how to tackle unfamiliar words that are not completely decodable (5.3)			
Read and spell less common alternative graphemes including trigraphs (5.4, 6.2)			
Read high and medium frequency words independently and automatically (5.5)			
Draw together ideas and information from across a text, using simple signposts in the text (7.1)			
Give some reasons why things happen or characters change (7.2)			
Use syntax and context to build their store of vocabulary when reading for meaning (7.4)			
Explore how particular words are used, including words and expressions with similar meanings (7.5)			
Read whole books on their own, choosing and justifying selections (8.1)			
Explain their reactions to texts, commenting on important aspects (8.3)			
Retell the main points of the story, explaining why things happened as they did			
Make inferences about characters' feelings and motives			
Make links between the feelings of characters and their own feelings			
Refer to other stories when discussing events and characters			
Express an opinion about what they like and dislike in stories			
Recognise that commas, exclamation marks and question marks show us how to read the text			
Explain the meaning of new vocabulary			
Children can apply their phonic skills and knowledge to recognise and spell an increasing number of complex words			
Children are secure with less common grapheme-phoneme correspondences, for example s/zh/			
Children can recognise phonic irregularities			

Stage 6 resources

To teach reading

- Stage 6 *Songbirds* and *eSongbirds*
- Oxford Reading Tree Stage 6 stories:

  Stage 6 *Stories*

  Stage 6 *More Stories Pack A*

  Stage 6 *More Stories Pack B*

  Stage 6 *More Stories Pack C*
- Oxford Reading Tree *MagicPage CD-ROM Stages 6–9*
- Stages 6–9 *Comprehension Photocopy Masters*
- Stage 6–7 *Story CDs*

For extra practice and consolidation

- Stage 6 *Floppy's Phonics*
- Stage 6–7 *Talking Stories*
- Stages 6–9 *Group Activity Sheets*
- Stages 1–9 *Phonics and Spelling Activities*
- Stage 6 *Workbooks 1, 2* and *3*
- *Games* Box 3
- *Oxford Reading Tree Online*

Further reading

- Stage 6 *Snapdragons*
- Stage 6 *Fireflies*
- Stage 5–6 *Glow-worms*
- *All Stars* Packs 2, 2A, 3 and 3A
- *Robins* Packs 1 and 3
- *Jackdaws* Packs 1, 2, 3
- *Traditional Tales* (age 7–8)

Stage 7 book recording chart

You can use this chart to record books as children read them. It also shows the key information on each book at a glance.

Group name/children's initials ....

Biff, Chip and Kipper stories

	Title	Date read	Main high frequency words (D = Decodable, T = Tricky)	NC level	Bookband level
St 7 Stories	The Broken Roof		**D**: about after again been books could don't fell funny long mend name old over find first climbed home house know mother saw silly sorry time three upset very picture your can't clothes new some; **T**: one through two who	Towards 2	Turquoise
	Lost in the Jungle		**D**: animals been catch bigger birthday home house jumped last lost made may over air angry behind called city jungle know lady love might mind placefull good have safe throw years saw shook so stay ten time took tree water way with found; **T**: through	Towards 2	Turquoise
	The Lost Key		**D**: about again air asked bed been could didn't don't called can't fast house flew found next last lost pictures would wouldn't round started threw make must saw seen sold sorry boy told; **T**: buy fault two	Towards 2	Turquoise
	Red Planet		**D**: about again came do don't down five from here home how just made may must over good little out safe saw so take some time want what took tree way water with called float floor; **T**: four one people pieces there were where	Towards 2	Turquoise
St 7 More Stories A	The Bully		**D**: about again against been boy came different do don't girl home just made new next over quickly frightened right saw trouble want know what ran take than that then very when with always called; **T**: friendly laugh two where your	Towards 2	Turquoise
	Chinese Adventure		**D**: about allowed back but came careful family has help lost made night not out put them time tomorrow other under worried would because very love new notice; **T**: fierce laughed one people two were	Towards 2	Turquoise
	The Hunt for Gold		**D**: back before boy else every from girl help home hungry just made much now off our out take than them excited little these three old time too us very when will with; **T**: bought brought buy money somewhere	Towards 2	Turquoise
	The Jigsaw Puzzle		**D**: angry back boy came clothes funny girl here luck must open quickly seen could knocked know little money secret them threw towards us very will with woman anything; **T**: caught library pieces question somewhere their	Towards 2	Turquoise
	The Motorway		**D**: about again between don't first good have here right house made painting surprise place woman wonderful pointed spoil these very when; **T**: build laugh people somewhere there where	Towards 2	Turquoise
	Roman Adventure		**D**: about angry back came first flat girl home horses interesting more nobody opened pleased race real smell street strong take tasted that them us very when will wish little nothing with watch would wrong because could cooked know; **T**: buy four heavy laughed one people soldiers	Towards 2	Turquoise
St 7 More Stories B	The Willow Pattern Plot		**D**: about by cruel came could loved called don't sound waited here house I'm saw time your; **T**: bought caught friends heard ready	Towards 2	Turquoise
	The Joke Machine		**D**: about terrible could don't here old put horses time very; **T**: centre guess laughed thought your	Towards 2	Turquoise
	Submarine Adventure		**D**: came could don't house amazing excited huge looked right wrong I'm make put; **T**: young your	Towards 2	Turquoise

Group name/children's initials ....

Biff, Chip and Kipper stories continued

	Title	Date read	Main high frequency words (D = Decodable, T = Tricky)	NC level	Bookband level
St 7 More Stories C	The Riddle Stone Part 1		**D**: after another black boy grandfather have help many more out some these trees want water way what with your; **T**: answer called colour half laugh question	Towards 2	Turquoise
	The Riddle Stone Part 2		**D**: after boys can't door help her how just last lives must dangerous first next one our out over ran saw seven that very what; **T**: answer half strange who were	Towards 2	Turquoise
	The Power Cut		**D**: beach black good help here last new now out put seen some take that then power surprise took us called first giant what ; **T**: busy hours laugh scary were	Towards 2	Turquoise
	The Big Breakfast		**D**: again call have home just last much must new energy next not now little out over some that then there took want what when with; **T**: juice laughed	Towards 2	Turquoise
	The Australian Adventure		**D**: after another been began being dream home air because dirty jump name new hundred voice water next out over rocks that them us wanted when; **T**: laugh	Towards 2	Turquoise

Fireflies

	Title	Date read	Main high frequency words (D = Decodable, T = Tricky)	NC level	Bookband level
St 7 Fireflies	Making a Space Shuttle		**D**: shuttle land empty tiles booster orbiter tank space spacecraft; **T**: Earth fuel engine people rocket	Within 2	Purple
	What Do You Want To Be?		**D**: astronaut teacher train ill swimmer coach officer dentist teeth some space Olympic; **T**: working doctor fashion designer firefighter electrician police special	Within 2	Purple
	Glorious Mud		**D**: mud soil different layers soaks experiment frame hut dry saucer jar sample pies water small; **T**: build types	Within 2	Gold
	Things that Sting		**D**: sting thread(s) animals plants bee jellyfish nettle body defend stingray painful tail poison scorpion kill person; **T**: dangerous	Within 2	Gold
	Fire		**D**: lightning forest town books fire cook start spread burned killed; **T**: people great damage library earthquake buildings	Within 2	Gold
	Sport Then and Now		**D**: sports balls heavy wore wear today made wet formal light wood long changed; **T**: equipment materials changes clothes	Towards 3	White

Snapdragons

	Title	Date read	Main high frequency words (D = Decodable, T = Tricky)	NC level	Bookband level
St 7 Snapdragons	Hero		**D**: went new with have jumped after sleep could children made night which little water; **T**: everyone please	Towards 2	Turquoise
	Toad Swims for his Life!		**D**: going down round began have head away last could come suddenly; **T**: other laugh	Towards 2	Turquoise
	The Monster Under the Stairs		**D**: monster know really under stairs could then wanted over have suddenly found; **T**: great laugh one	Towards 2	Turquoise
	Shy Shark		**D**: many very along dark down some over again little right; **T**: strange friends everyone there	Towards 2	Turquoise
	I'm Not Wearing That!		**D**: that always those night again children more different right little clothes; **T**: colour	Towards 2	Turquoise
	Rory's Lost His Voice		**D**: never stopped when coming more morning next couldn't down please voice because somewhere; **T**: can't where's friend	Towards 2	Turquoise

Stage 7 checklist of reading skills

Numbers in brackets refer to the Primary National Strategy *Literacy Framework* objectives, e.g. (8.2) means Strand 8, bullet point 2.

Group .... **Name** ....

Year 2 Reading skills	Autumn term	Spring term	Summer term
Read independently and with increasing fluency longer and less familiar texts (5.1)			
Know how to tackle unfamiliar words that are not completely decodable (5.3)			
Read and spell less common alternative graphemes including trigraphs (5.4, 6.2)			
Read high and medium frequency words independently and automatically (5.5)			
Draw together ideas and information from across a text, using simple signposts in the text (7.1)			
Give some reasons why things happen or characters change (7.2)			
Use syntax and context to build their store of vocabulary when reading for meaning (7.4)			
Explore how particular words are used, including words and expressions with similar meanings (7.5)			
Read whole books on their own, choosing and justifying selections (8.1)			
Explain their reactions to texts, commenting on important aspects (8.3)			
Allocate parts and read a play in a group, using sound effects and varied expression			
Retell the main points of a story, explaining why things happened as they did			
Make inferences about characters' feelings and motives			
Make links between the feelings of characters and their own feelings			
Refer to other stories when discussing events and characters			
Express an opinion about what they like and dislike in stories			
Recognise that commas, exclamation marks and question marks show us how to read the text			
Suggest alternative words for those used in the story			

Stage 7 resources

To teach reading

- Oxford Reading Tree Stage 7 stories:
  Stage 7 *Stories*
  Stage 7 *More Stories Pack A*
  Stage 7 *More Stories Pack B*
  Stage 7 *More Stories Pack C*
- Oxford Reading Tree *MagicPage CD-ROM Stages 6–9*
- Stages 6–9 *Comprehension Photocopy Masters*
- Stage 6–7 *Story CDs*

For extra practice and consolidation

- Stage 6–7 *Talking Stories*
- Stages 6–9 *Group Activity Sheets*
- Stages 1–9 *Phonics and Spelling Activities*
- Stage 7 *Workbooks 1* and *2*
- *Games* Box 3
- *Oxford Reading Tree Online*

Further reading

- Stage 7 *Snapdragons*
- Stage 7 *Fireflies*
- Stage 7–8 *Glow-worms*
- *All Stars* Packs 2, 2A, 3 and 3A
- *Robins* Packs 1 and 2
- *Jackdaws* Packs 1, 2, 3
- *Traditional Tales* (age 6–7)
- *Citizenship Stories*

Stage 8 book recording chart

You can use this chart to record books as children read them. It also shows the key information on each book at a glance.

Group name/children's initials ....

Biff, Chip and Kipper stories

	Title	Date read	Main high frequency words (D = Decodable, T = Tricky)	NC level	Bookband level
St 8 Stories	The Flying Carpet		**D**: afraid back called could hard made make much must new over please safely town very when with coming son because; **T**: already beautiful believe doesn't instead people someone thought through	Within 2	Purple
	The Kidnappers		**D**: been came catch different flew house how just last make must night over place pleased suddenly because another; **T**: beautiful busy everyone friends laughed lose many through working	Towards 2	Orange
	A Day in London		**D**: around called came easy first made much must next over second take than time took very wanted way money noise sight another because; **T**: bought brought everyone famous fierce heights instead people scene trouble worse	Within 2	Purple
	The Rainbow Machine		**D**: been better blue bright broken called could first good made must right seven suddenly three time two very when white with yellow because; **T**: any double field people straight though thought young worry	Within 2	Purple
	Victorian Adventure		**D**: allowed been first followed forever hard hungry light magic more much next street suddenly take television three time took; **T**: bought bread friends school shoe station taught trouble work	Within 2	Purple
	Viking Adventure		**D**: along came carried dark food found home magic middle more much noise our pleased wonder suddenly because idea; **T**: beautiful being either fierce school through	Towards 2	Turquoise
St 8 More Stories A	Egyptian Adventure		**D**: began amazing crushed climb knocked hissed jump last long seen strangers suddenly yelled; **T**: laugh scene special	Within 2	Purple
	Save Floppy!		**D**: began chest found next over push quickly shouted suddenly terrible these yelled because brother climb frightened powers giant idea; **T**: laugh rescued thought treasure once	Within 2	Purple
	Pocket Money		**D**: brilliant chart expensive groaned more extra little meeting millions idea reward photograph plastic pulled without; **T**: laugh once people	Within 2	Purple
	The Evil Genie		**D**: amazed bare been bottle asked because flew gasped escape wrecked hated last lived over pull suddenly terrible; **T**: genie ocean rescue treasure people	Within 2	Purple
	What Was It Like?		**D**: began from last after again another brother because been lived loud name pretend scared practice shelter sister sound stopped suddenly bomb; **T**: dangerous laugh once people scene thought	Within 2	Purple
	Flood!		**D**: across began bridge carry downstairs officer important next loud seen stop terrible upstairs another; **T**: brought canoe people thoughtful weather	Towards 2	Turquoise

Group name/children's initials ....

Fireflies

	Title	Date read	Main high frequency words (D = Decodable, T = Tricky)	NC level	Bookband level
St 8 Fireflies	Freaky Fish		**D**: fish eat eel sea bottom electric trumpet food spines teeth head; **T**: camouflage enemies colour(s)	Within 2	Purple
	Ice-Maker Ice-Breaker		**D**: sea(s) float(s) melt(s) hard frozen freeze ship(s) strong water iceberg ice; **T**: break(s)	Within 2	Gold
	Shipwrecks		**D**: ship sank trapped crew water survived shipwreck passengers; **T**: built famous people ocean treasure	Towards 3	White
	A Modern Day Explorer		**D**: balloon land attempt again problems flew days flight goal record launched weather solo tried; **T**: world	Towards 3	White
	Musician: Vanessa-Mae		**D**: when strings plays music type wood part(s) old modern bow sound(s) instrument good piano writes violin; **T**: world young	Towards 3	White
	What's Inside Me?		**D**: body lungs some brain gas blood oxygen; **T**: messages breathe heart muscles move works arteries veins	Towards 3	White

Snapdragons

	Title	Date read	Main high frequency words (D = Decodable, T = Tricky)	NC level	Bookband level
St 8 Snapdragons	More Little Mouse Deer Tales		**D**: again when please down because could would fast different really; **T**: through where everyone laughed thought somewhere	Within 2	Purple
	Jess and the Bean Root		**D**: lived very could magic couldn't again night going down suddenly something; **T**: thought through where's friend great	Within 2	Purple
	Big Liam, Little Liam		**D**: little night please shouted would couldn't what wanted dragon something know; **T**: their everyone friendly anyone laughed	Within 2	Purple
	The Band of Friends		**D**: head away some wanted what shouted would after window night looked around really; **T**: their friends everyone somewhere	Within 2	Purple
	Hair Scare		**D**: night wouldn't shouted couldn't grown some morning again something clothes wasn't round; **T**: everyone laughing school	Within 2	Purple
	Raju's Ride		**D**: children something clothes very cried morning; **T**: work school biscuit everyone their	Within 2	Purple

Stage 8 checklist of reading skills

Numbers in brackets refer to the Primary National Strategy *Literacy Framework* objectives, e.g. (8.2) means Strand 8, bullet point 2.

Group .... **Name** ....

Year 2 Reading skills	Autumn term	Spring term	Summer term
Read independently and with increasing fluency longer and less familiar texts (5.1)			
Know how to tackle unfamiliar words that are not completely decodable (5.3)			
Read and spell less common alternative graphemes including trigraphs (5.4, 6.2)			
Read high and medium frequency words independently and automatically (5.5)			
Draw together ideas and information from across a text, using simple signposts in the text (7.1)			
Give some reasons why things happen or characters change (7.2)			
Use syntax and context to build their store of vocabulary when reading for meaning (7.4)			
Explore how particular words are used, including words and expressions with similar meanings (7.5)			
Read whole books on their own, choosing and justifying selections (8.1)			
Explain their reactions to texts, commenting on important aspects (8.3)			
Allocate parts and read a play in a group, using sound effects and varied expression			
Retell the main points of a story, explaining why things happened as they did			
Make inferences about characters' feelings and motives			
Make links between the feelings of characters and their own feelings			
Refer to other stories when discussing events and characters			
Express an opinion about what they like and dislike in stories			
Recognise that commas, exclamation marks and question marks show us how to read the text			
Suggest alternative words for those used in the story			

Stage 8 resources

To teach reading

- Oxford Reading Tree Stage 8 stories:
  - Stage 8 *Stories*
  - Stage 8 *More Stories Pack A*
- Oxford Reading Tree *MagicPage CD-ROM Stages 6–9*
- Stages 6–9 *Comprehension Photocopy Masters*

For extra practice and consolidation

- Stages 8–9 *Talking Stories*
- Stages 6–9 *Group Activity Sheets*
- Stages 1–9 *Phonics and Spelling Activities*
- Stage 8 *Workbooks 1, 2* and *3*
- *Games* Box 3
- *Oxford Reading Tree Online*

Further reading

- Stage 8 *Snapdragons*
- Stage 8 *Fireflies*
- Stages 7–8 *Glow-worms*
- Stages 8–9 *Glow-worms*
- Stages 8–9 *True Stories* Pack 1
- *All Stars* Packs 2, 2A, 3 and 3A
- *Robins* Packs 2 and 3
- *Jackdaws* Packs 1, 2, 3
- *Traditional Tales* (age 7–8)
- *Citizenship Stories*

Stage 9 book recording chart

You can use this chart to record books as children read them. It also shows the key information on each book at a glance.

Group name/children's initials ....

Biff, Chip and Kipper stories

	Title	Date read	Main high frequency words (D = Decodable, T = Tricky)	NC level	Bookband level
St 9 Stories	Green Island		**D**: animals found interesting secret knew climbed dived our pushed sea study money washing waste engine adventure because; **T**: caught famous guitar island police school treasure walk worked	Within 2	Purple
	The Litter Queen		**D**: bottle because climbed control horrible hungry love posters prize queen screamed temperature tastes terrible sandwiches; **T**: centre countryside fields meadows special throughout	Towards 2	Turquoise
	The Quest		**D**: cracked flowers knight secret music terrible waste; **T**: beautiful believe castle crystal gnome journey meant	Within 2	Gold
	Storm Castle		**D**: bridge giant clever danger computer doorway lifted square middle monster much remembered; **T**: enormous favourite laughed school	Towards 2	Turquoise
	Superdog		**D**: drivers explored cheering city giant mistake quiet screamed service traffic themselves trousers; **T**: believe buildings hero minute rescue television yawned	Towards 2	Turquoise
	Survival Adventure		**D**: bandage chocolate opened surrounded village watched cruel quiet survival wander wonder worried; **T**: friendly honey journey	Within 2	Purple
St 9 More Stories A	The Blue Eye		**D**: after again could don't door first jumped man much covered must out over engine glowed pull ran that these took; **T**: aeroplane brought collection dangerous many one people thought	Within 2	Purple
	Rescue!		**D**: after again another been could doors first has home how last more next over ran take pilot wrecked that these us water would; **T**: aeroplane laughed many one people	Within 2	Purple
	Dutch Adventure		**D**: after again boy could did girl home how jump flood man more must over pulled ran take that these us water way wouldn't; **T**: bicycle half laughed one people thief worried	Towards 2	Turquoise
	The Finest in the Land		**D**: after again been boys could did girl good has home horse how last man must love next our ran saw three us way surprised would; **T**: castle daughter dungeons guitar many musicians one people	Within 2	Purple
	The Flying Machine		**D**: after another been could didn't first good has home engine huge how jumped last man must over rand wondered take these us water way would; **T**: aeroplane one pieces people straight	Towards 2	Turquoise
	Key Trouble		**D**: after again did different girl had has help home house frowned jumped last man more must next over take these took us water wouldn't; **T**: coloured grey laugh minutes naughty once tongue	Towards 2	Turquoise

Group name/children's initials ....

Fireflies

	Title	Date read	Main high frequency words (D = Decodable, T = Tricky)	NC level	Bookband level
St 9 Fireflies	Training Like an Athlete		**D**: athlete good ball very playing player(s) hot tennis football sport they training golf every makes competitive; **T**: won	Within 2	Gold
	Comic Illustrators		**D**: children picture(s)comic strip drew funny Roman drawing story illustrator newspaper idea; **T**: character stories famous people	Within 2	Gold
	Diamonds		**D**: deep mine miners rock hard cut polished used large smaller carat; **T**: diamonds weigh colour jewellery	Within 2	Gold
	Using a Computer		**D**: computer drawing smaller better first Internet change e-mail letter printer electricity text poster picture(s) photograph school; **T**: colour	Within 2	Gold
	Robots		**D**: robot job(s) movements arm(s) program box bulb holder control human; **T**: move instructions machine	Within 2	Gold
	Environmental Disasters		**D**: disasters oil spilled toxic gas nuclear smog kill animals water fish bird(s) firefighters spread(s) accident; **T**: pollution dangerous radioactive	Towards 3	White

Snapdragons

	Title	Date read	Main high frequency words (D = Decodable, T = Tricky)	NC level	Bookband level
St 9 Snapdragons	Mr Rabbit the Farmer		**D**: sometimes away only anything coming nothing; **T**: although neighbour enough flourishing businessman thought laughed worked furious feathery	Within 2	Gold
	Hot Dog		**D**: couldn't something morning around escape going some because determined museum; **T**: tough friends shoulders desperate measures restaurant laughed straight	Within 2	Gold
	King Donal's Secret		**D**: secret again another beloved tightly because climbed embarrassed; **T**: through everyone laugh guards unfortunate desperate	Within 2	Gold
	The Snow King		**D**: snow windows door around suddenly bright; **T**: daughter enough through straight although	Within 2	Gold
	Alien Swap		**D**: suddenly again window strange something what wasn't disgustingly expectantly; **T**: stomach believe through once wondered decision relieved great	Within 2	Gold
	Molly and the Giant		**D**: giant cried children window magic over something vanished; **T**: laughed proved enormous seized sword through	Within 2	Gold

Stage 9 checklist of reading skills

Numbers in brackets refer to the Primary National Strategy *Literacy Framework* objectives, e.g. (8.2) means Strand 8, bullet point 2.

Group .... **Name** ....

Year 2 Reading skills	Autumn term	Spring term	Summer term
Read independently and with increasing fluency longer and less familiar texts (5.1)			
Know how to tackle unfamiliar words that are not completely decodable (5.3)			
Read and spell less common alternative graphemes including trigraphs (5.4, 6.2)			
Read high and medium frequency words independently and automatically (5.5)			
Draw together ideas and information from across a text, using simple signposts in the text (7.1)			
Give some reasons why things happen or characters change (7.2)			
Use syntax and context to build their store of vocabulary when reading for meaning (7.4)			
Explore how particular words are used, including words and expressions with similar meanings (7.5)			
Read whole books on their own, choosing and justifying selections (8.1)			
Explain their reactions to texts, commenting on important aspects (8.3)			
Talk about stories they have read, and compare characters, settings and plots			
Retell the main points of a story, explaining why things happened as they did			
Make inferences about characters' feelings and motives			
Make links between the feelings of characters and their own feelings			
Express an opinion about what they like and dislike in stories			
Recognise that commas, question marks and exclamation marks show us how to read the text			
Notice how words change when prefixes or suffixes are added			

Stage 9 resources

To teach reading

- Oxford Reading Tree Stage 9 stories:
  - Stage 9 *Stories*
  - Stage 9 *More Stories Pack A*
- Oxford Reading Tree *MagicPage CD-ROM Stages 6–9*
- Stages 6–9 Comprehension Photocopy Masters

For extra practice and consolidation

- Stages 8 and 9 *Talking Stories*
- Stages 6–9 *Group Activity Sheets*
- Stages 1–9 *Phonics and Spelling Activities*
- Stage 9 *Workbooks 1, 2* and *3*
- *Games* Box 3
- *Oxford Reading Tree Online*

Further reading

- Stage 9 *Snapdragons*
- Stage 10 *Snapdragons*
- Stage 9 *Fireflies*
- Stage 10 *Snapdragons*
- Stages 8–9 *Glow-worms*
- Stages 10–11 *Glow-worms*
- Stages 8–9 *True Stories* Pack 1
- Stages 10–11 *True Stories* Pack 2
- *All Stars* Packs 2, 2A, 3 and 3A
- *Robins* Packs 2 and 3
- *Jackdaws* Packs 1, 2, 3
- *Traditional Tales* (age 7–8)
- *Citizenship Stories*
- *Treetops:*
  - *Stage 9 Fiction*
  - *More Stage 9 Pack A*

Oxford Reading Tree and the wider curriculum

The charts on the following pages show you where you can find specific Oxford Reading Tree resources to help you when you are teaching a particular cross-curricular topic or curriculum subject. There is also a series of charts showing how Oxford Reading Tree books relate to the text types recommended for each year group in the renewed Primary National Strategy *Literacy Framework*.

Oxford Reading Tree support for cross-curricular topics

A story is often the best way to introduce a cross-curricular theme or topic to a class. In talking about the story, and asking and answering questions, teachers can find out how much children already know and understand. For instance, at Stage 4 you could introduce a topic on Water by reading *Nobody Got Wet* (Stage 4 *Stories*) together. Follow-up questions naturally lead to things that float or sink in water, and where a river comes from and where it flows to. It begins to rain in the story, so that leads to talk about the water cycle, and the splash from the puddle gives another example of surface water.

In each chart there are easier titles that children can read or use as a stimulus for writing at a given level, and stories from later stages that a teacher might like to use in story time. The books from the very early stages are useful in Years 1 (P2) and 2 (P3) as starting points for writing. Children can be asked to provide the text for the wordless story books at Stage 1 or provide extended stories. Where there are appropriate *Glow-worms* poetry books, these are also listed, together with non-fiction titles from the *Fireflies* series'.

Titles in bold print are available as Big Books.

Abbreviations

Numbers in brackets show Stage

A,B or C mean More Stories Packs A, B or C

FW: First Words
PS: Patterned Stories
MPS A: More Patterned Stories Pack A
BCS: Biff and Chip Storybooks
FS: First Sentences
Sn: Snapdragons
MFW: More First Words
MPS: More Patterned Stories
FPh: First Phonics
Sp: Sparrows
MFS: More First Sentences

Stages 1 and 1+ cross-curricular topics

Ourselves

Read and write	Read together	Story time
Getting up (1)	Kipper's Birthday (2A)	Kipper's Idea (3A)
The Haircut (1)	Spots (2A)	Midge in Hospital (3 Sp)
Kipper's Diary (1+ FS)	The Wobbly Tooth (2B Kipper's Laces (2B)	It's Not Fair (5A)
Making Faces (1+ MPS)		The New Baby (5B)
Look After Me (1+ MFS A)		
Going Up and Down (1+ Sn)		
Poems: Glow-Worms: Out and About Poems(1+—2); Body poems(3–4); Movement poems(3–4)		
Non-fiction: Fireflies: This is Me(1+); Hop, Skip and Jump(1+ M); How to Draw Yourself(3)		

Friends and Family

Read and write	Read together	Story time
Six in a Bed (1 FW)	**A New Dog (2)**	**Nobody Wanted to Play (3)**
Fun at the Beach (1 FW)	**The Go-Kart (2)**	The Wedding (4A)
Hide and Seek (1+ FS)	The Babysitter (2A)	Nobody Got Wet (4A)
Good Old Mum (1+ PS)		Everyone Got Wet (4B)
Who Did That? (1+ MPS)		Look Smart (4C)
Can You See me? (FPh)		Gran (5)
My Dad (1+ Sn)		Christmas Adventure (6A)
Hello Grandma! (1+ Sn)		
Poems: Glow-Worms: Family poems (1+—2)		
Non-fiction: Fireflies: Maya's family (1+)		

Animals

Read and write	Read together	Story time
The Hedgehog (1)	**A New Dog (2)**	The Chase (2B)
Floppy Floppy (1 FW)	**What a Bad Dog (2)**	Floppy the Hero (2B)
Floppy Did This (1 MFW)	Creepy Crawly (2 PS)	**A Cat in the Tree (3)**
Go Away Floppy (1+)	The Lost Puppy (2 MPSA)	Pip at the Zoo (3 Sp)
What Dogs Like (1+ A)	What Is It? (2 MPSA)	Pip and the Little Monkey (3 Sp)
Go Away Cat (M1+ A)	Poor Floppy (2 FPh)	Don't be Silly (6B)
Top Dog (MFS1+ A)	Put it Back (2 FPh)	
Floppy's Bone (1+ MFSB)	Tortoise! Tortoise! (2 Sn)	
The Pet Shop (1 PS)		
My Dog Needs a Bone (1+ Sn)		
Poems: Glow-Worms: Animal poems 1+—2); Pet poems (5–) Farm poems (5–6) Fox poems (8–9)		

Stage 2 cross-curricular topics

	Read and write	Read together	Story time
Celebrations	Presents for Mum (2 FPh)	**The Toys' Party (2)**	The Wedding (4A)
	The Band (2 MPSA)	Kipper's Birthday (2A)	Look Smart (4A)
	The Animal Party (2 Sn)	The Carnival (3B)	The New Baby (5B)
			Christmas Adventure (6A)
	Poems: Glow-Worms: Party poems (1+—2) Special Days poems (5–6)		
	Non-fiction: Fireflies: Shopping for a Party (2); How to Make a Fruit Salad (4M)		

	Read and write	Read together	Story time
Hands and Feet	Big Feet (1+)	**New Trainers (2)**	Poor Old Mum (4A)
	Look At Me (1+)	Kipper's Laces (2B)	Tug of War (4C)
	See Me Skip (1+ FPh)	The Ice Rink (3 FPh)	The Adventure Park (5C)
		Midge in Hospital (3 Sp)	Dad's Run (5C)
	Poems: Glow-Worms: Body Poems (3–4)		
	Non-fiction: Fireflies: Boots and Shoes (2M) Animal Feet (4M) Ballet (4M)		

	Read and write	Read together	Story time
Pushing and Pulling	Push! (1+ PS)	**The Go-Kart (2)**	Adam's car (4 Sp)
	Hook a Duck (1+ MFS B)	**By the Stream (3)**	Nobody Got Wet (4A)
	Melting Snow (1+ Sn)	**The Rope Swing (3)**	The Go-Kart Race (6A)
	Poems: Glow-Worms: Movement poems (3–4) Transport poems; Machine poems (7–8)		
	Non-fiction: Fireflies: Push and Pull (2M)		

Stage 3 cross-curricular topics

	Read and write	Read together	Story time
Food	**The Toys' Party (2)**	The Barbecue (3B)	Rotten Apples (6A)
	Kipper's Birthday (2 MS A)	Strawberry Jam (3A)	Roman Adventure (7A)
			Victorian Adventure (8)
			Viking Adventure (8)
			Batter Splatter! (6 Sn)
			Dutch Adventure (9A)
			The Sandwich that Jack Made (5 Sn)
	Poems: Glow-Worms: Food poems (5–6)		
	Non-fiction: Fireflies: Making Muffins (1+) Shopping for a party (2) How to Make a Fruit Salad (4M) From Curry to Rice (4) Food as Art (6)		

	Read and write	Read together	Story time
Light and Dark	The Hedgehog (1 BCS)	The Storm (4)	The Magic Key (5)
			Underground Adventure (5A)
			A Fright in the Night (6A)
			The Mole Who Was Scared of the Dark (6 Sn)
			The Power Cut (7A)
			The Monster Under the Stairs (7 Sn)
	Poems: Glow-Worms: Night poems (11) Star poems (1–11) Special Days poems (5–6)		
	Non-fiction: Fireflies: Night animals (4)		

	Read and write	Read together	Story time
Hot and Cold	The Water Fight (2A)	The Cold Day (3B)	Village in the Snow (5)
	Big Feet (1+)	The Snowman (3A)	Safari Adventure (5C)
	The Ice Cream (1+FPh)	The Ice Rink (3 FPh)	Lost in the Jungle (7)
		Melting Snow (3 Sn)	Christmas Adventure (6A)
			Hot Dog (9 Sn)
	Poems: Glow-Worms: Weather poems (1+–2) Snow poems (10–11) Seasons poems (5–6)		
	Non-fiction: Fireflies: Hot and Cold (2) Fire (7) Ice Maker, Ice Breaker (8) Survival (10) Volcanoes (5M)		

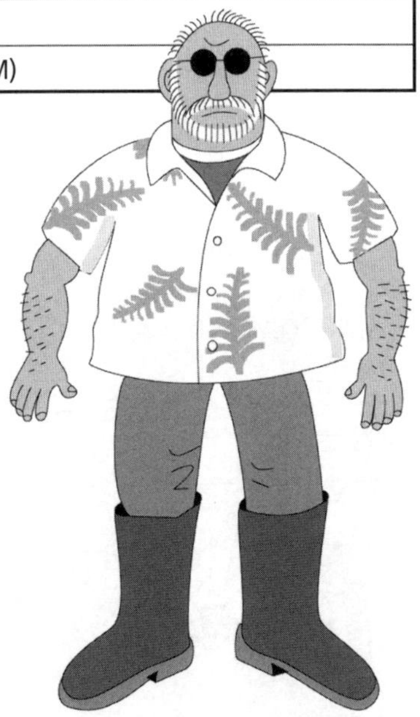

Stage 4 cross-curricular topics

Our School	Read and write	Read together	Story time
	Book Week (3B)	The Play (4)	A New Classroom (5B)
	The Carnival (3B)	The Storm (4)	The Outing (6)
	The Steel Band (3 FPh)	The Dragon Dance (4B)	Don't be Silly (6B)
	At School (1)	Mosque School (4 Sp)	The Broken Roof (7)
			The Bully (7A)
			The School Trip (5 Sn)
	Poems: Glow-Worms: Alphabet poems; Number poems (3–4)		
	Non-fiction: Fireflies: Our Class (2) The School Band (3M)		

Water	Read and write	Read together	Story time
	The Water Fight (2A)	Nobody Got Wet (4A)	A Monster Mistake (5A)
	The Rope Swing (3)	Everyone Got Wet (4B)	Mum to the Rescue (5B)
	The Cold day (3B)		Flood! (8A)
	At the Pool (3B)		Toad Swims for his Life! (7 Sn)
	The Mud Bath (3 FPh)		
	Pond Dipping (3 Ph)		
	Little Mouse Deer and the Crocodile (4 Sn)		
	Poems: Glow-Worms: Snow poems (10–11) Water poems (7–8) Weather poems (1+—2)		
	Non-fiction: Fireflies: On the Beach (1+M) Floating Boats (3M) The Seaside Then and Now (5M); Freaky Fish (8) Sharks (5M)		

Houses and Homes	Read and write	Read together	Story time
	Biff's Aeroplane (2B)	House for Sale (4)	The Broken Roof (7)
	The Barbecue (3B)	The New House (4)	Survival Adventure (9)
	A House for Hedgehog (3 Sn)	Come In! (4)	Locked Out (5 Sn)
		The Camcorder (4A)	Alien Swap (9 Sn)
		The Den (4C)	
	Poems: Glow-Worms: Castle poems (10-11) Family Poems (1+-2)		
	Non-fiction: Fireflies: Houses Then and Now (5) Shells (4) How to Make a Wormery (5M)		

Stage 5 cross-curricular topics

	Read and write	Read together	Story time
Living in the past		The Whatsit (5) It's Not Fair (5A)	The Broken Roof (7) Roman Adventure (7A) I'm Not Wearing That! (7 Sn) Victorian Adventure (8) Viking Adventure (8) What was it Like? (8A) Dutch Adventure (9A) Key Trouble (9A)
	Poems: Glow-Worms: Castle Poems (10) Pirate poems (10–11)		
	Non-fiction: Fireflies: Romans (10) Sport Then and Now (7) The Seaside Then and Now (5M) Grandad and Me (4)		

	Read and write	Read together	Story time
Holidays	**On the Sand (3)** **By the Stream (3)** Pip at the Zoo (3 Sp) Nobody Got Wet (3A)	Gran (5) Village in the Snow (5) A Monster Mistake (5A) Camping Adventure (5B) The Adventure Park (5C) Safari Adventure (5C)	Christmas Adventure (6A) The Motorway (7A) A Day in London (8) Green Island (9)
	Poems: Glow-Worms: Sea poems (8–9) Farm poems (5–6) Special Days poems (5–6)		
	Non-fiction: Fireflies: The Seaside Then and Now (5M)		

	Read and write	Read together	Story time
Growing	The Haircut (1) Look at Me (1+) Look After Me (1+) Kipper's Birthday (2A) The Lost Puppy (2 PSA) The Little Dragon (2 PSA) Kipper's Laces (2B) Sniff (3 FPh)	The Magic Key (5) The New Baby (5B)	In the Garden (6) Kipper and the Giant (6) Hair Scare (8 Sn)
	Poems: Glow-Worms: Seed poems (10–11) Egg poems (8–9) Body poems (3–4)		
	Non-fiction: Fireflies: Odd Eggs (10)		

Stage 6 cross-curricular topics

	Read and write	Read together	Story time
Dinosaurs	Big Feet (1+)	The Outing (6)	
		Land of the Dinosaurs (6)	
	Poems: Glow-Worms: Monster poems (11)		
	Non-fiction: Fireflies: Dinosaurs (6)		

	Read and write	Read together	Story time
Shapes and Sizes	Big Feet (1+)	In the garden (6)	Molly and the Giant (9 Sn)
	Creepy-crawly (2 PS)	Kipper and the Giant (6)	Big Liam, Little Liam (8 Sn)
	The Big Egg (2 FPh)	The Treasure chest (6)	
	The Hole in the Sand (2 FPh)	The Shiny Key (6)	
	The Best Sandcastle (2 Sn)	Something Big (6 Sn)	
	Bull's Eye! (3B)		
	Little Mouse Deer and the Crocodile (4 Sn)		
	The Whatsit (5)		
	Little Dragon (5 Sn)		
	Poems: Glow-Worms: Seed poems (10–11) Giant poems (8–9)		
	Non-fiction: Fireflies: Big and Little (1+) Shapes (4) Freaky Fish (8) Big Cats (4M)		

	Read and write	Read together	Story time
What is it made from?	The Balloon (4A)	The Treasure Chest (6)	Red Planet (7)
	The Dragon Dance (4B)	The Shiny Key (6A)	The Lost Key (7)
	The Scarf (4B)	Mirror Island (6B)	The Broken Roof (7)
	The Flying Elephant (4B)	The House that Jack Built (6 Sn)	The Motorway (7A)
	The Magic Key (5)		The Hunt for Gold (7A)
	The Sandwich that Jack Made (5 Sn)		The Joke Machine (7B)
			The Rainbow Machine (8)
	Poems: Glow-Worms: Food poems (5–6)		
	Non-fiction: Fireflies: Making a Book (10) Building a Road (3M) How to Make a Fruit Salad (4M) How to Make a Puppet Theatre (4M) How to Make a Wormery (5M) Making a Space Shuttle (7) Making Muffins (1+)		

Stage 7 cross-curricular topics

	Read and write	Read together	Story time
The Sun and the	The Water Fight (2A)	Red Planet (7)	Jackdaws Anthologies: Space and Planets
	Poems: Glow-Worms: Star poems (10–11) Space poems (8–9)		
	Non-fiction: Fireflies: Making a Space Shuttle (7)		

	Read and write	Read together	Story time
Wild World	New trees (2 MPSA)	Lost in the Jungle (7)	Green Island (9)
	Safari Adventure (5C)	Shy Shark (7 Sn)	Survival Adventure (9)
	Land of the Dinosaurs (6)		Jess and the Bean Root (8S n)
	In the Garden (6)		The Snow King (9 Sn)
	Poems: Glow-Worms: Fox poems (8–9) Monkey poems (10–11) Dragon poems (10–11) Monster poems (11) Minibeast poems (7–8) Mouse poems (11)		
	Non-fiction: Fireflies: Things that Sting (7) Night Animals (4) Jumpers (M3) Sharks (M5) Unusual Birds (M5) Big Cats (M4) Animal Faces (1+M) Dinosaurs (6) Freaky Fish (8)		

	Read and write	Read together	Story time
Wheels	Look at me (1+)	The Hunt for Gold (7A)	A Day in London (8)
	One Wheel (1+B)	The Motorway (7A)	The Rainbow machine (8)
	The Go-Kart (2)		The Flying Machine (9A)
	Joe and the Bike (3 Sp)		
	Adam's Car (4 Sp)		
	The Great Race (5A)		
	The Go-Kart race (6A)		
	Poems: Glow-Worms: Transport poems (7–8) Machine poems (7–8)		
	Non-fiction: Fireflies: Tour de France (6) Going somewhere (3) Transport (2) Wheels (1+) Diggers (M2) The Fire Engine (1+M)		

Stage 8 cross-curricular topics

	Read and write	Read together	Story time
Sounds	Robin Hood (6)	A Day in London (8)	The Finest in the Land (9a)
	The Steel Band (3 FPh)	The Rainbow Machine (8)	Tom the Whistling Wonder (10Sn)
	The Band (2PSA)	The Band of Friends (8Sn)	
	What a Din (1+ FPh)		
	Rory's Lost His Voice (7 Sn)		
	The Headache (1+ PS)		
	Poems: Glow-Worms: Music poems (7–8) Sounds poems (3–4)		
	Non-fiction: Fireflies: Musician: Vanessa Mae (8) World Instruments (4) The School Band (M3)		

	Read and write	Read together	Story time
Where I live	House for Sale (4)	A Day in London (8)	Survival Adventure (9)
	The New House (4)		Dutch Adventure (9A)
	Hero (7 Sn)		
	The Motorway (7)		
	Poems: Glow-Worms: Shopping poems (5–6) Farm poems (5–6) Sea poems (8–9)		
	Non-fiction: Fireflies: Houses Then and Now (5)		

	Read and write	Read together	Story time
Mini-beasts	Creepy-crawly (2 PS)		Green Island (9)
	What is it? (2 PSA)		
	Put it Back (2 FPh)		
	Book Week (3B)		
	Pond Dipping (3 FPh)		
	The Mouse with No Name (4 Sn)		
	In the Garden (6)		
	Poems: Glow-Worms: Minibeast poems (7–8)		
	Non-fiction: Fireflies: How to Make a Wormery (5M)		

Stage 9 cross-curricular topics

	Read and write	Read together	Story time
Keeping fit	See Me Skip (1 FPh)	Survival Adventure (9)	A Proper Bike (Robins 1)
	Reds and Blues (1+)		Hamid Does His best (Robins 3)
	Go On Mum!(1+A)		Games and races (Jackdaws Anthologies 2)
	At the Pool (3B)		
	The Mud Bath (3 FPh)		
	Tug of War (4C)		
	The Adventure Park (5C)		
	Alf Saves the Day (5Sn)		
	Dad's Run (5C)		
	Poems: Glow-Worms: Sports poems (11) Movement poems (3–4)		
	Non-fiction: Fireflies: Survival (10) Training like an Athlete (9) Sport Now and Then (7) Skateboarding (6) Ballet (4 M) How to be Healthy (3) Football, Football (3)		

	Read and write	Read together	Story time
Our World	Flood (8A)	Green Island (9)	Seas and Storms (Jackdaws Anthologies 2)
	Submarine Adventure (7B)	The Litter Queen (9)	Snow and Ice (Jackdaws Anthologies 3)
	Lost in the Jungle (7)		Winter Stars (Jackdaws Anthologies 3)
	Safari Adventure (5C)		
	Poems: Glow-Worms: Star poems (10–11)		
	Non-fiction: Fireflies: Environmental Disasters (9) Modern Day Explorer (8) Unusual Buildings (6) Wonders of the World (5) Volcanoes (5M) The Seaside (5M) Building a Road (3M)		

	Read and write	Read together	Story time
Technology	Red Planet (7)	Storm Castle (9)	The Emergency (Robins 1)
	The Rainbow machine (8)		The Photograph (Robins 2)
	The Whatsit (5A)		
	The Camcorder (4A)		
	Chip's Robot (1+B)		
	Poems: Glow-Worms: Machine poems (7–8)		
	Fireflies: Working in the Film Industry (10) Using a Computer (9) Robots (9) Hello! (4M)		

Oxford Reading Tree links with curriculum subjects

Many of the Oxford Reading Tree books at Stages 1–9 can be used to support teaching in a range of curriculum subjects. You can use the books shown below, when you are teaching the relevant curriculum area, for independent reading or in story time, depending on the stage of the book and the reading ability of the children.

The lists below give an idea of the connections it is possible to make with curriculum subjects – but they are not exhaustive and you will find many other potential links as you get to know and use the books in your classroom.

Abbreviations
Numbers in brackets show Stage
A, B or C mean More Stories Packs A, B or C

PS: Patterned stories
FF: Fireflies
FPh: First Phonics
MPS A: More Patterned Stories Pack A
MFF: More Fireflies

History
Grandad and Me (4 FF)
Houses Then and Now (5 FF)
The Seaside Then and Now (5 MFF)
Sport Then and Now (7 FF)
Roman Adventure (7A)
Victorian Adventure (8)
Viking Adventure (8)
Egyptian Adventure (8A)
What Was It Like? (8A) (Second World War)

Geography
Going Somewhere (3 FF)
Wonders of the World (5 FF)
Volcanoes (5 MFF)
Safari Adventure (5C)
Wild Weather (6 FF)
Lost in the Jungle (7)
Chinese Adventure (7A)
A Day in London (8)
Flood! (8A)
Environmental Disasters (9 FF)
Dutch Adventure (9A)

Science
Hot and Cold (2 FF)
Push and Pull (2 MFF)
A Sinking Feeling (2 PS) (floating and sinking)
It's the Weather (2 PS) (weather)
New Trees (2 MPS A) (planting trees)
What Is It? (2 MPS A) (identifying animals)
Spots! (2A) (being ill)
How to be Healthy (3 FF)
Floating Boats (3 MFF)
Pond Dipping (3 FPh)
Looking After Your Dog (5 FF)
In the Garden (6) (close-up view of garden plants and creatures)
Submarine Adventure (7B) (life under the sea)

Design and Technology
Wheels (1+ FF)
Making a Space Shuttle (7 FF)
Using a Computer (9 FF)

Links with the Literacy Framework suggested text types

These charts show examples of books in Oxford Reading Tree that link well with the suggested text type planning modules for Year 1 (P2) and Year 2 (P3). For more information on the planning modules, see
http://www.standards.dfes.gov.uk/primaryframeworks/literacy/planning/Year1/
and
http://www.standards.dfes.gov.uk/primaryframeworks/literacy/planning/Year2/

Abbreviations
Numbers in brackets show Stage
A,B or C mean More Stories Packs A, B or C

FF: Fireflies
Sn: Snapdragons
MFF: More Fireflies
GW: Glow-worms

Year 1 text types

	Text type	Oxford Reading Tree books
Narrative	Familiar settings	All the core Biff, Chip and Kipper books at Stages 3–5 have a familiar setting and context
	Predictable and patterned language	Most core Biff, Chip and Kipper books and Snapdragon books at Stages 3–5 have predictable and patterned language. Specific examples include: New Blue Shoes (3 Sn) A House for Hedgehog (3 Sn) Mr Fox's Socks (4 Sn) The Sandwich that Jack Made (5 Sn)
	Stories from a range of cultures	Little Mouse Deer and the Crocodile (4 Sn) The Tortoise and the Baboon (4 Sn) The Chatterbox Turtle (5 Sn)
	Traditional/Fairy tales	The Singing Bird (3 Sn) Little Mouse Deer and the Crocodile (4 Sn) The Tortoise and the Baboon (4 Sn) The Chatterbox Turtle (5 Sn) Sleeping Beauty (5C)
	Fantasy worlds	The Magic Key stories from Stage 5 provide a good introduction to fantasy stories, e.g: The Dragon Tree (5) Vanishing Cream (5A) Kipper and the Trolls (5C) Drawing Adventure (5C) In addition: Little Dragon (5 Sn)

	Text type	Oxford Reading Tree books
Non-fiction	Labels, lists and captions	There are labels and captions in most Fireflies Non-fiction books at Stages 3–5, including: My Week (3 FF) Shapes (4 FF) World Instruments (4 FF) Houses Then and Now (5 FF)
	Instructions	How to Draw Yourself (3 FF) How to Be Healthy (3 FF) Looking After Your Dog (5 FF) Magic Tricks (5 FF)
	Dictionary	From Curry to Rice – A Food Dictionary (4 FF)
	Information texts	All Fireflies Non-fiction books at Stages 3–5, including: Football, Football! (3 FF) Choices (3 FF) Night Animals (4 FF) Shells (4 FF) Public Art (5 FF) Wonders of the World (5 FF)
	Recounts	My Week (3 FF) Grandad and Me (4 FF) E-mails Home (5 FF)

	Text type	Oxford Reading Tree books
Poetry	Senses	Colour Poems (3–4 GW) Sounds Poems (3–4 GW) Food Poems (5–6 GW)
	Pattern and rhyme	All Glow-worms collections at Stages 3–4 and 5–6 include many examples of poems with strong patterns and rhyme.
	Poems on a theme	All Glow-worms collections at Stages 3–4 and 5–6 are arranged by theme. At Stages 3–4 the themes are Alphabet Poems, Body Poems, Colour Poems, Movement Poems, Number Poems and Sounds Poems. At Stages 5–6 the themes are Farm Poems, Food Poems, Pet Poems, Seasons Poems, Special Days Poems and Shopping Poems.

Year 2 text types

	Text type	Oxford Reading Tree books
Narrative	Familiar settings	All the core Biff, Chip and Kipper books at Stages 6–9 have a familiar setting and context. In addition: Sam Sorts it Out (6 Sn) Batter Splatter! (6 Sn) I'm Not Wearing That! (6 Sn) Rory's Lost His Voice (6 Sn) Big Liam, Little Liam (8 Sn)
	Traditional stories	Stories with a similar structure and language to traditional stories include: The Mole who was Scared of the Dark (6 Sn) The Band of Friends (8 Sn) Mr Rabbit the Farmer (9 Sn) The Snow King (9 Sn) Molly and the Giant (9 Sn) King Donal's Secret (9 Sn)
	Different stories by the same author	All of the core Biff, Chip and Kipper stories are written by Roderick Hunt, so children can look for similarities and differences in style across a range of his books.
	Stories by significant authors	Snapdragons have a wealth of authors such as Geraldine McCaughren (e.g. Stage 9 The Snow King), Malachy Doyle (e.g. Stage 8 The Hair Scare), Monica Hughes (Stage 8 More Little Mouse Deer Tales). ORT True stories include authors such as Alison Hawes, Tony Bradman, Maureen Haselhurst and Paul Shipton.

	Text type	Oxford Reading Tree books
Non-fiction	Instructions	Making a Space Shuttle (7 FF) Training Like an Athlete (9 FF) Using a Computer (9 FF)
	Explanations	Wild Weather (6 FF) What's Inside Me (8 FF) Environmental Disasters (9 FF)
	Information texts	All Fireflies Non-fiction books at Stages 6–9, including: Food as Art (6 FF) Glorious Mud (7 FF) Ice-Maker Ice-Breaker (8 FF) Comic Illustrators (9 FF)
	Non-chronological reports	Dinosaurs (6 FF) Skateboarding (6 FF) Unusual Buildings (6 FF) Things that Sting (7 FF) Fire (7 FF) Freaky Fish (8 FF) Shipwrecks (8 FF) Diamonds (9 FF) Robots (9 FF)

	Text type	Oxford Reading Tree books
Poetry	Patterns on the page	All Glow-worms collections at Stages 7–8 and 8–9 include many examples of poems with interesting shapes and patterns, and where the words are arranged on the page to particular effect.
	Really looking	Minibeast Poems (7–8 GW) Senses Poems (7–8 GW) Water Poems (7–8 GW) Egg Poems (8–9 GW) Sea Poems (8–9 GW)
	Silly stuff	Machine Poems (7–8 GW) Music Poems (7–8 GW) Giant Poems (8–9 GW) Space Poems (8–9 GW) Wizard Poems (8–9 GW)

Reading at Home with Oxford Reading Tree

Research has shown that the support and practice that children gain from reading at home has a markedly beneficial effect upon their progress. Reading at home builds confidence, fluency and enjoyment of books. It also creates a shared pleasurable learning experience for children and parents.

The books that children take home may be selected from a box at a suitable level, or chosen as suitable by the teacher. In either case you may need to explain to parents that the emphasis is on reading for fun and practice, not on testing or a need to read impressively difficult books.

You may decide to send home books that have been read in shared and guided reading sessions, for further practice. Alternatively you can select titles from the 'More Stories' at each stage for those children who seem to pick up new vocabulary effortlessly, and can therefore approach a new text at the appropriate level with confidence.

Supporting parents

- You may decide to have a meeting at the beginning of each school year to discuss your approach to reading, and suggest ways in which parents can support their children. At such a meeting you can demonstrate how to make the most of the opportunity to share a book with a child.
- Recently published Oxford Reading Tree stories have notes for parents inside the front and back covers. These notes give detailed suggestions on how to approach the book, how to support reading, and ideas for follow-up activities.
- There is also a guide for parents called At *Home with Oxford Reading Tree*. This can be downloaded free of charge from www.OxfordPrimary.com or purchased in bulk.
- To accompany the schoolbooks parents may also wish to introduce their children to the Oxford Reading Tree *Read at Home* series, a carefully levelled, brand new set of stories designed for parents to read with their children. A useful handbook *Helping your child to read* and *Flashcards* are also available. See the website for more information www.oup.com/oxed/children/readathome/.

On the next page you will find photocopiable bookmarks with brief notes for parents. The suggestions are related to the Oxford Reading Tree Stages. A bookmark can be sent home inside the book. Parents can write notes about the child's response on the back of the bookmark.

Reading at home bookmarks

Name ____________

Date ____________

Title ____________

Stages 1, 1+, 2

I love stories. I hope you like this one.

- Choose somewhere quiet and comfy to sit, and try to ignore all distractions!
- Talk about what is happening in the pictures. Praise your child for noticing details.
- Talk about anything the story reminds you of.
- Always finish with praise for everything the child has done well.

Name ____________

Date ____________

Title ____________

Stages 3, 4, 5

This is one of my favourite stories. Which is your favourite?

- Choose a quiet time and place where you and your child can both concentrate.
- Remind your child to run his or her finger under the print while reading.
- Help your child to use letter sounds to read any new words.
- Give encouragement all the time.
- At the end, talk about the story. Find the parts you both liked best.

Name ____________

Date ____________

Title ____________

Stages 6, 7, 8, 9

I love the magic key. It takes us to amazing places.

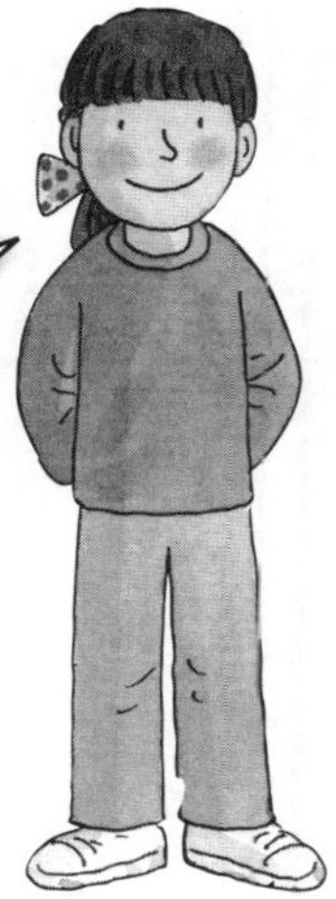

- Choose a quiet time and place where you and your child can both concentrate.
- Do not feel you must finish the whole story. Use this bookmark to keep your place for tomorrow.
- Encourage your child to try to work out new words. Help if necessary.
- Praise your child for reading with expression.
- Talk about particular incidents that were funny, exciting, or true to life.

Notes